The Fountain of Youth at Red Boiling Springs, Tennessee: Part 2

By

CL Gammon

𝔇𝔯𝔭

LAFAYETTE, TENNESSEE
deepreadpress@gmail.com

First Deep Read Press Edition.

Published in the United States of America

Edited by: Kim Gammon

Cover Design by: Kim Gammon

Cover Photo by: Kim Gammon

Paperback ISBN: 978-1-954989-58-0

Published by:
DEEP READ PRESS
Lafayette, Tennessee
www.deepreadpress.com
deepreadpress@gmail.com

For the good folk of Red Boiling Springs, Tennessee.

Contents

Introduction

There are many myths and legends surrounding the discovery of what is now called Red Boiling Springs, Tennessee. One goes that around 1830, a solidary hunter named Edmund Jennings went out early in the season. He was an experienced hunter and he felt confident that he would soon find an abundance of game. Jennings followed well-worn animal trails for several days and they led him into what is now eastern Macon County, Tennessee.

After days of tracking, Jennings stood at the crest of a hill and looked down at a lush valley with a large stream running through it. His heart raced when he saw what every professional hunter of those times longed to see – a large salt lick. Animals of all kinds crowded around the lick competing for the salt that had settled there.

The valley was already well-known to Native Americans. There was a Cherokee village led by Chief Katawley not far from the salt lick.

When Jennings returned home he spread the news about the lovely valley with the salt lick where even the worst hunter could bag as much game as he wanted. The news enticed several families to pull up stakes, move there, and establish a settlement.

The new settlers began pushing out the old and there were several pitched battles between the whites and the Natives before the Natives were gone.

"Aunt" Sukie Goad is usually credited with being the first to discover and open the Red Boiling Springs. But her contributions did not stop there. She was an institution at the resort that prospered there. She also made an excellent salve and she sold box after box to visitors who purchased it as much because Aunt Sukie made it than for any particular use they have had for it.

This, the second volume in the series, follows certain aspects of Red Boiling Springs from the dawn of the 20th Century until the end of 1945. It is broken down into 10 chapters, each of which looks at one facet of the resort town.

The events dealt with in each chapter are presented in rough chronological order and with as little overlapping as possible.

Many famous and important people frequented Red Boiling Springs during the period covered by this book. They included Congressmen, Governors, a Speaker of the United States House of Representatives, a future American Secretary of State, and jazz legend Earl Hines. The book isn't just about the rich and famous, however. Scores of local merchants, teachers, and others receive rightful mention within these pages.

Every effort possibile has been made to ensure and verify the accuracy of the information presented here. However, sometimes spellings of names and other facts vary from source to source. When this occurred, I have accepted the most reliable source available.

While the modern spelling is "sulfur" for many years it was spelled "sulphur." I use the modern spelling except when quoting statements from older sources when "sulphur" was used.

It is my hope that you enjoy this book, and if you should learn something too, that will just be gravy.

1. The Miracle Water

Red Boiling Springs became known for its mineral waters at least as early as 1850, and its reputation continued to grow for the next century. The water was so popular that it was regarded as something of a natural patent medicine. Because of its waters, Red Boiling Springs was considered as a modern-day fountain of youth and thousands came there annually to regain their health. Thousands of others purchased the water at drugstores in Nashville or elsewhere or had it delivered to their homes and businesses.

This chapter looks at the efforts to market the water and relates the high regard that the public and medical personnel had for it.

April 8, 1900. Demoville & Company located across the Street from the Maxwell House in Nashville had distributed Red Boiling Springs water in Nashville since at least 1892. (see *The Fountain of Youth at Red Boiling Springs, Tennessee, Part 1*). Demoville & Company managers pointed out to their customers the importance of drinking pure water. They contended, "The subject of mineral water is receiving more attention every year by the medical profession as well as by the thinking public. The many serious troubles caused by impure waters are too numerous to mention. When you decide to use a mineral water, it is important to get it as fresh as possible."

The water could be had at the store from the soda fountain. Demoville & Company would also deliver it in Nashville or ship it anywhere in the United States. Customers could place orders by telephone by dialing 66.

May 10, 1901. The "Red Boiling Water Company" received a charter for the purpose of "developing and exploiting the waters of the Red Boiling Springs of Macon County." Five Nashville entrepreneurs headed the corporation: William L. Dudley, B. Kirk Rankin, W. E. Buist, George Trabue, and Charles Trabue. The company had capital stock of $5,000 (more than $180,000 in today's currency).

June 16, 1901. The Red Boiling Water Company was working hard marketing its product. The owners stated, "We control the famous Red Boiling Springs, Macon County, Tennessee, and we are now prepared to deliver the water to consumers anywhere in Nashville or elsewhere in quart bottles only. Every bottle is filled at the spring and the water reaches the consumer in perfect condition. The Red water is the greatest kidney and bladder remedy on earth. Ask your doctor." One could order a dozen quart bottles of the water by telephoning 2527. Or one could pick it up in person at the company headquarters at 311 Church Street in Nashville.

The Red Boiling Water Company was also trying to line up "druggists and dealers" in Nashville and surrounding towns to act as retail agents for the famous water. The water company offered "attractively labeled" pint bottles of water exclusively to dealers. The water retailed for 10¢ per pint bottle (the price in 1901 currency was about equivalent to what soft drinks cost today).

The company promised that its water would help everyone that was "out of sorts. You know it. If you don't, ask your doctor."

June 23, 1901. The Red Boiling Water Company clarified some things. It reminded consumers that "For fifty years or more the waters of Red Boiling Springs, Macon County, Tennessee have been famous for their wonderful curative values. Not until now has a business-like effort been made to bottle the water with care at the spring and introduce it in all parts of the country. The company controls the sale of Red Boiling Springs water absolutely."

The water company related to potential customers that it maintained "offices and storerooms at 311 Church Street, and from this depot deliveries will be made in Nashville or to any part of the country without delay." The water company offered a newly published free booklet describing both its waters (red and black) and presented "the opinion of some of the best doctors you know. They say Red Boiling is the best mineral water in the world for certain conditions."

The company reiterated that its water was "put up in two sizes of bottles only – pints and quarts. The pints can be had by consumers at soda water fountains and where mineral waters are sold at retail only. They sell for 10 cents. The quarts are for family use and are delivered anywhere in the city limits in cases of one dozen."

The Red Boiling Springs Water Company took pride in its bottling operation. Its owners said, "We have made every arrangement for bottling Red Boiling Water in as careful and attractive a manner as any mineral water in the world, and we wish especially to call attention to the fact that every label carries a guarantee that the bottle was filled at the spring. The water thus reaches the consumer practically without coming in contact with the air."

The water company's owners concluded by telling consumers why they should drink the Red Boiling Springs water: "If you have the habit of getting sick when the hot weather comes on, begin drinking Red Boiling water, and you will find it easy to keep well. It flushes the entire system and prevents clogging of the internal human machinery.

"If you are sick, it will make you well. If you are half sick it will make you as good as new."

In truth, Red Boiling Springs water had been marketed in Nashville for decades. However, the Red Boiling Water Company was the first organization whose only purpose was to sell water from the resort town.

July 17, 1901. The Red Boiling Water Company cautioned Nashville residents that city wells and springs "breed disease and most municipalities close them." The proprietors of the water company continued, "It is said that there are two thousand springs and wells within the city of Nashville from which people drink water. From some of them, water is sold in jugs. In the best

9

regulated cities these sources of water supply are closed by ordinance in the interest of public health as the unavoidable seepage from sewers, etc., makes water of this kind a first-class vehicle for typhoid and similar diseases."

Then the company leaders explained why Nashville citizens should purchase and drink Red Boiling Springs water. "Purity is only one of the virtues of Red Boiling Springs Water. The fact that the bottles are filled in the wilds of Macon County twenty-five miles from a railroad, insures this. But its remarkable action in kidney and bladder troubles – Bright's disease, diabetes, gravel [kidney stones, bladder stones, and gall stones], cystitis, dropsy, etc. – gives it great fame as medicinal water. Another beauty of Red Boiling Water is the fact that it is tasteless."

Company owners admitted that their water was "not as cheap as jug sulphur," but they added quickly "it costs only half as much as Buffalo Litha or Poland and is more valuable than either. Ask your doctor."

Buffalo Lithia water was bottled at Buffalo Lithia Springs, Virginia. At its peak, Buffalo Lithia was sold at about 20,000 locations in the United States, Canada, and Europe. Poland Spring water was bottled in Poland, Maine. Today, water carrying the Poland Spring brand is sold by Nestle.

The Red Boiling Water Company repeated that it sold a dozen quart bottles of its water for $2 and that it would pay customers for the empty bottles they returned.

In this instance being off the beaten path was a benefit to Red Boiling Springs. In those days, railroads used coal as fuel for their engines. Coal dust pollutes everything from the air to the waterways. The fact that it was free from pollution was a great selling point for Red Boiling Springs water.

July 21, 1901. The Red Boiling Water Company actively sought testimonials. They received a good one from the Tennessee Superintendent of Public Instruction, Morgan C. Fitzpatrick. Fitzpatrick wrote, "I have visited Red Boiling Springs for a number of years and have also used the bottled water. I consider the water unexcelled by any other for kidney and like complaint."

July 30, 1901. The Red Boiling Water Company reminded customers of its prices. It charged "$2.00 per dozen quarts or $2.40 for a case of two dozen pints, delivered." Consumers would receive 25¢ for returning a dozen empty quart bottles and 40¢ for returning a case of empty pint bottles.

August 1, 1901. Davidson County, Tennessee Sheriff B. Lewis Hurt presented a testimonial for Red Boiling Springs water: "I have used Red Boiling Springs Water and regard it by far the best water in the state. It is not only efficacious in kidney and bladder troubles, but I deem it superior for building up a run-down constitution or invigorating an overworked man. I am glad arrangements have been made to furnish the bottled water to those who cannot afford the time or expense of going to the springs, and believe it will prove very popular."

Another testimonial came from Davidson County Criminal Court Clerk, R. A. Milam: "I take pleasure in recommending the use of Red Boiling Springs Water to my friends for I regard it as an elixir of life. I have used it and found relief in its virtues. I not only know it is to be beneficial for kidney, bladder and kindred complaints, but regard it as a most excellent remedy for stomach troubles, as well as a tonic for toning up the general system. I know no water which is its superior."

August 2, 1901. The managers of the Red Boiling Water Company continued the drumbeat for their product. They contended "the way to get quick and lasting benefit from the use of Red Boiling Water" was to drink it at home and at work. The company representatives stated, "When a man goes to the springs and notes improvement in his appetite and general health at the end of a week's steady use of the water he is well pleased.

"It often happens that this same man will order a case of Red Boiling water sent to his home, drink one bottle a day until one case is gone and then quit."

Next came a caution: "Now, we have claimed all along that Red Boiling Water is the best mineral water on the market, and we have the testimony of a lot of doctors to back this claim, but we

11

don't claim that the water used as indicated above will cure anything amounting to a disease."

August 11, 1901. The Red Boiling Water Company released a "Full explanation of uses of two kinds of Red Boiling water, Black sulphur and the Red." The explanation began, "Only those who have been to the Macon County springs seem to understand the difference between the black and red waters that are being placed on the market by the Red Boiling Water Company of this city [Nashville].

"Briefly stated, it is this: The black water tastes very strongly of sulphur and is a purgative which acts gently with the permanent beneficial results on the liver and bowels. It is recommended, generally speaking, for all derangements of the liver and stomach.

"The red water is almost tasteless and is a very free diuretic which acts quickly on the kidneys and gives rapid relief in any suffering due to disorder of the kidney, bladder and urinary channels.

"Indigestion and resulting insomnia can be certainly cured by use of the black water. In this connection the case of former Mayor [J. B.] Donelson of Gallatin is interesting."

Donelson stated, "I was afflicted with a chronic and aggravated case of indigestion, had suffered intense agony for years and had tried all the various waters of the country without avail, besides taking a prodigious amount of medicine. I drank the black sulphur water ten days, and at the end of that time, my digestion was splendid and my sleep sweet and refreshing."

The explanation continued, "It has been proven beyond a doubt by many excellent physicians that the red water dissolves gravel [kidney stones] and causes it to be discharged in the shape of sand. It has also been used with great success in various stages of Bright's disease and diabetes, causing all traces of albumen to disappear."

The writer meant albumin, not albumen. Albumin is a protein in the blood that decreases in diabetics. At the time, the reduction of albumin was thought to be a positive. We know now that the opposite is true.

Mr. Cook of Louisville added his story: "I was advised by my physician, Dr. Richard Douglas, of Nashville, to go to Red Boiling Springs. My life was despaired of. It made me like a new man, bringing 50 percent of albumen down to but the slightest trace."

The explanation ended with, "The Red Boiling Water Company wishes especially to assure those who have been to the springs that the water is bottled from the two springs in the park just across just across from the hotel that was burned several years ago. [See *The Fountain of Youth at Red Boiling Springs, Tennessee: Part 1.*] The bottling is done under the supervision of an attaché of one of the scientific departments of Vanderbilt University, and the water is now delivered to consumers just as it comes from the spring."

August 15, 1901. The Red Boiling Water Company relayed to the public that sulfur was "not necessarily a sign of value" in mineral water. "A great many people have an idea that any water that has sulphur taste possesses valuable medicinal properties and that all sulphur water is alike. This is a great mistake. The black water from Red Boiling Springs for instance, possesses curative powers greater than any other water having sulphur taste. The sulphur is simply an accident and is not the cause of this water's great reputation in the treatment of the stomach, liver and bowel troubles.

"The Red Water from these springs is practically tasteless and yet it has a deserved reputation greater than any water, whether it has a taste, contains lithia, or what not, for curing kidney and bladder troubles and toning up the system generally.

"Taste has nothing to do with the medicinal value of water. Results alone count. Ask your doctor about Red Boiling Water, either Red or Black, or send for our booklet which contains statements from the best doctors you know."

Lithia water is a type of mineral water that contains lithium salts such as carbonate, chloride, or citrate of lithium. Early versions of soft drinks such as Coca-Cola and 7-Up were made with lithia water.

September 1, 1901. The Red Boiling Water Company was promoting its water everywhere. The company shared a letter from a woman who believed "Her only hope of recovery rests on a famous Tennessee mineral water." The woman, who lived "within a very short distance of the most celebrated health resorts and lithia springs in Virginia," wrote a letter stating: "Please send four dozen bottles of Red Boiling Water at once, without letting one day pass by, for my only hope of recovery from this painful disease of gravel is in this water."

The company related that "A great many Nashville people have an idea that a mineral water from Virginia or New York or Maine is necessarily better than any water Tennessee can produce.

"The Red Boiling Water Company is proving the fallacy of this idea every day by shipping Red Boiling Water into the heart of the most famous lithia water fields of other states.

"For dissolving calculi and absolutely curing such cases as this Virginia lady writes of Red Boiling Water has a record of success superior to that of any known mineral water."

September 10, 1901. As part of the "Grand Carnaval of the Jolly Elks" they were sponsoring, the Nashville chapter of the Elks Club was renting about 200 booths to vendors. The Red Boiling Water Company secured one of the booths.

May 18, 1902. There were some complaints about the cost of the water from Red Boiling Springs. To counter the complaints, the Red Boiling Water Company sought to explain why its water was more expensive than other mineral waters were: "You know that Red Boiling Water is the most valuable mineral water for the treatment of kidney, bladder and stomach troubles. You have heard this all your life. You also know it costs more to put this water on the market than any other, because the springs are 25 miles from the railroad. So, if it costs more than some others, it is *worth* more. No man who is sick can afford to have anything but the *best*. Neither can his wife and children. Try a ten-cent bottle at the soda fountain, or wherever you drink."

The company promised to deliver the water by the case, anywhere within a radius of 100 miles of Nashville. The company's phone number remained 2527, but its address was now at 154 North Cherry Street in Nashville.

June 15, 1902. The Red Boiling Water Company claimed its water was the "most valuable" and "the most popular" on the market. It also reminded Nashvillians that the hotel at the springs was accepting visitors.

June 19, 1902. The Red Boiling Water Company was offering a "special price" on orders of three cases or more of its water.

August 17, 1902. The Red Boiling Water Company took to calling its water "nature's greatest prescription" and was offering to deliver it "in cases of two dozen pints or one dozen quarts."

March 14, 1906. Called the "Sample Store," a charity venture of the Young Women's Guild of the Vine Street Christian Church opened on Church Street in Nashville. The nonprofit enterprise sold donated items including Red Boiling Springs water provided by Demoville & Company.

August 9, 1906. The United States Geological Survey headquartered in our nation's capital issued a bulletin regarding mineral water in the United States. Naturally, the bulletin was of interest to the folk in Red Boiling Springs.

The findings indicated that mineral water production declined "considerably" in the United States during 1905. The decline was especially marked in New York, California, and Massachusetts. Conversely, mineral water output was "greatly increased" in Indiana, Minnesota, Pennsylvania, Tennessee, Texas, and to a lesser degree in Alabama.

The survey differentiated between mineral water consumed for medicinal purposes, that used as a "table" drink, and water used for bathing. It made perfect sense that in those areas that large amounts of mineral water were used at home as a table drink the overall consumption was higher than in those places where it was used for medicinal purposes only.

The survey also considered the relative prices of mineral water. In the Northern states, the price was usually 25¢ or more per gallon, while in the South it routinely sold for 10¢ or less per gallon.

The survey predicted a "steady healthy growth" in mineral water production, but insisted that few people visited summer resorts for the water alone. For cold water resorts to compete and survive, amid the heavy competition, they had to provide visitors with superior recreational facilities, great accommodations, and first-class dining at a reasonable price. Otherwise, pleasure-seekers would go elsewhere.

May 18, 1909. Robert McEwen was proud of the resort at Red Boiling Springs, and he didn't mind saying so. He told the public that Red Boiling Springs had "been famous as a health resort for 100 years." McEwen pointed out again that "These waters continue to effect almost miraculous cures." He then recounted the diseases he alleged the waters cured: "Gravel, calculus, in the kidneys, bladder, and gall bladder, Bright's disease, diabetes, inflammation of the bladder and urethra, rheumatism, dyspepsia, habitual constipation, dropsy, and diseases peculiar to women." He also offered all that wanted one, a free booklet "giving the experiences of dozens of physicians of the highest repute who have used these waters in their practice."

McEwen finished by repeating that his water possessed "the most valuable curative agents in most diseases of the kidneys, liver, stomach and bladder in America, if not in the world."

July 29, 1916. The management at Cloyd Place bragged that its waters were still famous for the "marvelous cures" they effected. The owner of Cloyd Place, the Red Boiling Springs Company, stated that its springs were "at the head of the fountains of these waters." The management continued, "The four natural springs of the Red Boiling Springs Company are Deer Lick, Salt Lick, Silver Spring, and the celebrated Herculean Spring, known as

Double and Twist. The waters of these springs have proved of marvelous efficacy in relieving and curing diseases of the stomach, kidney, bowel, bladder, and the treatment of rheumatism and constipation."

The Red Boiling Springs Company was taking advantage of its water by bottling it and shipping it to customers. Or it could be bought in Nashville at Jungermann's Store. Jungermann's was located at 527-529 Church Street and sold a wide array of groceries as well as hot lunches, ice cream, and soft drinks. The store opened at 6:30 a.m. and closed at 11:30 p. m.

September 11, 1916. Cloyd Place promoters claimed its "waters are Nature's own healing potions, and a month will rebuild the most run-down machine." The promoters continued that "The healing powers of RED BOILING SPRINGS have cured hundreds of cases of rheumatism, stomach trouble, kidney and bladder disease."

February 28, 1917. The Red Boiling Springs Company formed a new company called the Red Boiling Springs Distilling Company. The company had capital stock of $2,000 (almost $53,000 in today's currency). What exactly it intended to distill wasn't revealed, but it had to do with the water at Red Boiling Springs.

October 26, 1920. The proprietor of Cloyd Place addressed Nashvillians, "We wish to call your attention to the fact that we have opened an office at 161 Fourth Avenue North, Room 10, Steger Building for the sale of the Cloyd Place Red Boiling Springs water. These waters need no introduction as they have been known for many years for their health-giving properties."

The proprietor recommended the "concentrated Herculean water" for gallstones, constipation, liver, and stomach troubles. He also made a point of saying that the concentrated Herculean water wasn't fortified with any other substance. The waters of "Deer Lick" were recommended for rheumatism and "kidney trouble."

The waters were guaranteed to be bottled at the springs by the Red Boiling Springs Company.

July 20, 1924. The management of the Arlington Hotel at Red Boiling Springs touted the "red, white, and black water in the yard; also freestone water." They also pointed out that they owned the "Little Red Well" at Red Boiling Springs.

February 17, 1925. R. & O. Drugstore was an agent for Red Boiling Springs water in Nashville. The drugstore's motto was "Why not be safe and drink mineral water this summer?"

July 12, 1925. After decades on the market, the waters of the famous Red Boiling Springs had not lost any of their popularity. The common belief was that the medicinal powers of the waters were equaled only in "the most celebrated health resorts in Europe."

May 4, 1928. The J. R. Smith Water Company was selling Red Boiling Springs water at its Nashville location. The company declared, "The world's greatest physician is coming to Nashville in the name of Red Boiling Springs mineral waters – Red, Black, Sampson." The company received the water from Red Boiling Springs daily and sold it in cases of 24 one pint bottles. The company would deliver it to homes or businesses for those that didn't want to pick it up at the store.

The J. R. Smith Company guaranteed that if used as directed it would cure all forms of stomach, bladder, and kidney troubles, as well as Bright's Disease, diabetes, gallstones, diseased prostate glands, constipation, rheumatism, kidney stones, malaria, eczema, and "diseases peculiar to women." The company also promised to provide an analysis and free consultation upon request.

June 23, 1928. One of the first health stores in Nashville, the Tennessee Health Food Company announced its grand opening at 727 Church Street. Company owners Frank Unger and J. E.

Waldrum stated proudly that they sold three varieties of Red Boiling Springs water "for the state of Tennessee." The company delivered the water to homes and businesses everywhere, but one could also purchase it with other health food products at the store.

March 24, 1929. Albert Henry Counts, known as Henry, of the Palace Hotel told prospective visitors, "If you are suffering from the aftereffects of influenza, you'll find our black and red sulphur water will help you regain your strength and tone up your nervous system. The original black and red sulphur wells are only a short distance from the hotel and are free to all guests."

May 14, 1929. The Young-Thompson Drug Company located in Nashville at 718 Church Street announced that it was an agent for Red Boiling Springs water. The company's motto was "Buy the Best."

July 18, 1932. The water from Red Boiling Springs had lost none of its reputation. It was still considered a real world fountain of youth. The belief was that in the previous half century "literally thousands [had] gone there, partaken of the water and departed with health restored." The revived patrons of the water often made a pilgrimage to the springs an annual event.

Sufferers came from "Maine to California" to use the water from the "oasis" at Red Boiling Springs to recuperate. Reputedly, the health giving water was "described by physicians and analytical chemists as containing all the elements necessary to be a balanced mineral water." For instance, Picard Laboratories of Brimingham, Alabama issued an analysis of the black water from the spring at the Donoho Hotel. The report stated, "This is a sulphur magnesia water of decided medicinal properties ... We think that the black sulphur water is fine, as it should have decided purgative action from the large amount of magnesia present. This, with the hydrogen sulfide [is] good for gastro-intestinal trouble."

July 24, 1932. The resort could also provide a testimonial from a medical professional as to the value of its waters. Dr. H. C. Hesson praised the water: "Having been the resident physician at Red Boiling Springs for the past twenty-eight years I am pleased to give my testimony to the public regarding the efficacy of these waters. Thousands of cases have come under my supervision and I have witnessed many remarkable cures of kidney, bladder, liver and stomach diseases in their many forms, rheumatism, skin diseases, etc.

"I feel no hesitancy in saying to the medical profession: 'Send us your hard cases and let us cure them.' And to the people: 'Come and be cured.'"

Other testimonials swore that "Hundreds of cases have come to hand where supposedly hopeless cases were sent there only to have a permanent cure effected in a remarkably short space of time."

The Palace Hotel management contended that its "red" water was especially recommended for "Bright's Disease, diabetes, rheumatism, and hemorrhages from kidneys and bladder." The "black" water, so said hotel management, was "good for gallstones, catarrhal condition [inflammation] of gall bladder, stomach trouble and chronic constipation."

The white sulfur water at the Moss Hotel was used to treat dyspepsia (indigestion). The white water was believed to almost always effect a cure.

July 9, 1933. The staff of the Hotel Lincoln touted the fact that every year, hundreds of visitors took advantage of the "bodybuilding properties" of its famous red and black sulfur waters.

The Donoho Hotel offered four types of water that its management promised would bring one "back to glowing health."

2. At the Resort

The resort at Red Boiling Springs gained in popularity and grew to be world famous. While most of the visitors to the resort town lived in Tennessee (especially Nashville), and Kentucky, visitors came from practically everywhere. This chapter looks at the resort and some of the hotels that operated there. It also deals with the competition the hotels faced and the efforts managers made to improve their facilities in order to keep their guests coming year after year.

March 23, 1900. Henry Moss of Union City, Tennessee was 60 and he suffered from Bright's disease. He traveled halfway across the state to Red Boiling Springs hoping to improve his health. Sadly, after being at Red Boiling Springs for just a few days, the disease overcame Moss and he passed away.

April 26, 1900. Merlin A. West, of Lafayette, Tennessee, who was 18, married Eunice Wakefield, age 21, at Red Boiling Springs. West was the son of former State Representative Jesse West. Wakefield was the daughter of Issac Newton "Bose" Wakefield. Merlin West would later serve in the State Senate.

June 7, 1900. Cloyd Place in Red Boiling Springs was filling up. Most of the 30 odd guests there were from Kentucky and Tennessee, but some of those staying there were from places such as Bridgeport, Alabama, and Durham, North Carolina.

Meanwhile, John H. Sabens continued to operate the "old reliable resort" at Red Boiling Springs. Sabens told potential guests that his resort was "open year-round for those seeking health." He repeated that the waters there were especially good for "liver and stomach trouble." He reminded those living in the hot cities that his resort "situated on the Highland Rim, Macon

County, Tennessee" [was] cool and pleasant." Sabens promised that at Red Boiling Springs the "cuisine and service [was] good." He finished by stating that hacks met the trains in surrounding towns and transported pleasure seekers to the resort. For those considering a trip to his resort, he offered to mail them a catalog with rates, etc.

June 13, 1900. Thomas Tyler Cloyd operated "the popular health and pleasure resort" called Cloyd Place. He recommended his "ideal retreat" for its "high elevation [and] pure air." He then recounted the health benefits of the waters at Red Boiling Springs, saying they could "cure dropsy, rheumatism, diseases of the stomach, liver and genitourinary organs." Cloyd advised the sick that if they came to Red Boiling Springs they would be "avoiding the surgeon's knife."

Genitourinary diseases include congenital abnormalities, iatrogenic injuries, and disorders such as cancer, trauma, infection, and inflammation. The proponents of mineral water truly believed that it would cure those diseases.

July 17, 1900. There were more than 30 new arrivals to Cloyd Place, some from as far away as Jacksonville, Floridia and Atlanta, Georgia.

July 30, 1900. The were almost 30 new guests at Red Boiling Springs. One family came from Kingston, Georgia.

August 4, 1900. There were about 20 new guests staying at Cloyd Place. They were all from Kentucky and Tennessee.

August 11, 1900. Cloyd Place continued filling up. In the past week, the hotel had registered about 50 new guests. They were all from Kentucky and Tennessee.

September 5, 1900. Red Boiling Springs remained a destination for newlyweds. R. L. Preston and his bride, the former

Daisy High, returned to their Woodbury, Tennessee home after honeymooning in Red Boiling Springs.

September 15, 1900. Webb Bennett, C. L. Moffatt, and Moffatt's son returned the 250 miles or so to Troy, Tennessee after their vacation in Red Boiling Springs.

May 29, 1901. The competition among resorts was growing fiercer all the time. Red Boiling Springs was one of 19 resort towns "in the highlands and mountains of Tennessee" that were on or near the Nashville, Chattanooga & St. Louis Railroad line. All the resorts offered "Cool Nights! Pure, Fresh Air! Mineral Waters! Magnificent Breezes!" The challenge to a resort was to set itself apart from all the others. Red Boiling Spring had the advantage of its great reputation, but that only went so far.

June 9, 1901. Cloyd Place claimed to offer the "best water in the world." Cloyd touted its varieties of water: "Red Boiling, Black Boiling, and Black Sulphur, of the very strongest." Cloyd Place offered a free booklet to anyone who was interested in learning more.

July 26, 1901. Reports were that Cloyd Place was "in the midst of its most prosperous year." There were more than 50 guests at the hotel from Kentucky and Tennessee alone.

Beyond the healthy influx of vacationers at the hotel, since the previous summer, Thomas Tyler Cloyd had "'smitten the rock' and opened up a new well, which flows 6,000 gallons of water per day of the highest strength, floating over 800 grains of solids to the gallon making it one of the best medicated waters in existence."

Mr. and Mrs. Walter Johnson, and Mrs. C. W. Jarrell, all of Shelbyville, Tennessee were among those summering at Red Boiling Springs.

September 10, 1901. Thomas Tyler Cloyd reported that Cloyd Place had room for 20 to 30 more guests. He added that after September 10, room rates would be only $5.25 per week.

August 19, 1902. Dero A. Stalker of Hartsville, Tennessee and Frances Foley of Lebanon, Tennessee temporarily left Red Boiling Springs and rode to Lafayette, Tennessee for the purpose of being married. Upon their arrival, without leaving their buggy, Reverend W. H. Carter performed their wedding ceremony. The happy couple then turned their buggy around and returned to Red Boiling Springs for their honeymoon.

August 21, 1902. Prominent Marion County, Tennessee attorney, B. E. Tatum and his family were enroute to Red Boiling Springs for a little rest and relaxation.

January 25, 1903. The Epson Springs (formerly Epperson Springs) resort in western Macon County had been in intense competition with Red Boiling Springs since before the Civil War. In 1903, Epson Springs was for sale, or lease. The resort had done a healthy business for many years and even though it was aged, it had much to offer. It was only three miles from the railroad at Westmoreland. Besides that, its owners said, "It consists of the wonderful black, white, and red sulphur, chalybeate and freestone springs of national reputation for their curative properties. The hotel [features] ten large rooms, a large dining room and kitchen, are well-furnished and equipped in good order for hotel purposes. In addition to this there are cottages with about forty rooms, all furnished; [a] large ballroom, splendid bowling alley and servants' quarters are located so as not to be any annoyance to the invalids. This property contains 420 acres of land, 300 acres in fine timber and 100 acres in use for farm, garden and hotel purposes." Harris Brown and W. J. Morrison of Nashville oversaw the sale.

The west Macon County resort was not finished, not by a long shot. It reopened, saw a reversion to the name Epperson Springs, and remained in operation for several more decades.

May 16, 1903. The large crowds coming to Red Boiling Springs every season coupled with the intense competition from other resorts made constant improvement and expansion of hotels a necessity. S. S. Kemp, the manager of the Red Boiling Springs Hotel informed the public that during the past winter "we have erected a number of new rooms, including a large dining room." He continued that the hotel was "now prepared to provide comfortably" for everyone that wanted to stay there. He added that all the rooms were "newly furnished."

May 23, 1903. George R. Knox, General Freight Agent of the Nashville, Chattanooga & St. Louis Railroad was at Red Boiling Springs "for his health." He had been under a doctor's care for several days who related that Knox was "almost broken in health." Knox returned to Nashville and immediately went back to work on June 4 "with his normal strength and vitality restored."

September 9, 1903. S. S. Kemp related to the public that "autumn is the best time to go to this famous health resort. The water removes the debilitating effects of summer." Kemp added that his hotel had a "good table" and an "excellent livery" stable.

December 13, 1903. The Red Boiling Springs Hotel accepted guests even in the colder months. This was good news for Albert Franklin, horse trainer for John J. Greener & Company. Franklin left Nashville and made his way to Red Boiling Springs for a vacation.

April 6, 1904. S. S. Kemp announced that the Red Boiling Springs Hotel was open and accepting guests. He encouraged prospective guests to write or telephone for rates and other information.

June 15, 1904. Thomas Tyler Cloyd reminded the public that "Cloyd Place or Upper Red Boiling Springs is at the head of the FOUNTAIN for the famous RED BOILING SPRINGS WATER; ten of the best springs and wells in the locality, varying in strength

[from] very mild to that holding in solution 868 grains of mineral medicine to the U. S. gallon."

(Note: According to the Environmental Protection Agency and Center for Disease Control, drinking water containing high amounts of sulfates can cause diarrhea, especially in infants.)

Cloyd proclaimed proudly that "Our original Red Boiling Spring, formerly known as Whitney Spring, has cured its tens of thousands."

Cloyd also confirmed that Cloyd Place was open year round, and that Dr. J. M. Mellon was the resident physician during the summer.

June 18, 1904. General George W. Gordon of Memphis was the Commander of the Tennessee Division of the United Confederate Veterans. On June 17, General Gordon was the Grand Marshall of the Confederate Reunion Parade in Nashville. The next day, he departed for a vacation at Red Boiling Springs for one week.

During the Civil War, General Gordon was wounded and captured at the Battle of Franklin.

July 24, 1904. S. S. Kemp, manager of the "old original" Red Boiling Springs, continued try to improve his hotel and outclass the other nearby resorts, especially his competition in his hometown. Kemp announced that he had "completed and furnished twenty additional new cabins, also a new bath house." He also touted the "first-class barber service ... various amusements on the grounds and a good livery" stable at his resort. Kemp promised "Accommodations for all the guest who may desire to visit."

August 25, 1904. S. S. Kemp told interested parties, "The best time of the year to visit this resort is in August and September. The Red Boiling Springs Hotel (the lower spring, the old original) is open the year round, with plenty of room for all comers." Kemp reminded potential vacationers that the resort had new cottages, bath house and bowling alley."

May 26, 1905. S. S. Kemp related to the public that "The old original Red Boiling Springs Hotel is now open for guests." Kemp promised vacationers that he had made "new improvements" including "a first-class bath house." He encouraged the doubtful to "Ask your physician about these famous springs."

June 21, 1905. The following ad appeared in *The Nashville American*: "Wanted: An experienced middle-aged lady to superintend the kitchen and dining-room at a summer resort that has about 100 guests at a time; must have good references. Address Box 5, Red Boiling Springs, Tennessee."

July 12, 1905. Squire Obediah Donoho told prospective pleasure seekers that "Donoho's Red Boiling Springs is located just above the old original, and considered far superior to any in this vicinity." Donoho continued that his resort had "added to our amusements" including a "ballroom, ten pin alley, and bath house." Donoho informed those considering a trip to his hotel that "Our conveyances will be at Carthage Tuesdays, Thursdays, and Saturdays."

About the Donoho Hotel: A hotel owner named Whitley built the first hotel on what is now the Donoho property sometime after 1890. Around 1901, the first Donoho hotel was built on the property by Whitley's son-in-law, Squire Obediah Donoho (1863–1908). Donoho's family had operated a general store in Red Boiling Springs before then. After Donoho's death, the hotel and property passed into the hands of Whitley's daughter, Tennessee D. "Tennie" Whitley, and her husband, Brady Chitwood (1875–1958). The first Donoho Hotel burned in 1915, and the following year the Chitwoods built the present hotel building as a replacement.

August 12, 1905. J. F. Jenkins, Nashville City Passenger Agent of the Tennessee Central Railroad had returned from a stay at Red Boiling Spring. He went "for the benefit of his health" and reported that he was "much improved."

November 5, 1905. S. S. Kemp continued to tout the "original Red Boiling Springs resort." He told the public that at Red Boiling Springs "the water and climate are at their best in November. A visit now will put you in good condition for winter."

January 3, 1906. James F. O'Shaughnessy had formed the Red Boiling Springs Company on December 15, 1889, and had purchased the resort. O'Shaughnessy leased the resort to Joseph M. (Joe) Dedman and Dedman operated the resort until 1898 when he took over operation of Bailey Springs in Alabama.

At some point, O'Shaughnessy sold the resort to Dedman. Dedman still owed O'Shaughnessy $40,000. Dedman defaulted and Nashville attorney Charles C. Trabue, acting on behalf of O'Shaughnessy, filed a complaint in the US Circuit Court, asking that the court foreclose on Dedman and the Red Boiling Springs Company unless Dedman could come up with the $40,000 principal and additional interest he owed O'Shaughnessy.

On June 16, the US Circuit Court granted the foreclosure decree against Joe Dedman and the Red Boiling Springs Company. The judge then placed the Red Boiling Springs Company property up for auction. The auction was held in Nashville and O'Shaughnessy's attorney, Charles C. Trabue placed a bid of $15,000 for his employer and "bought" it for O'Shaughnessy at its assessed value.

Most observers believed that O'Shaughnessy would lease the resort.

May 25, 1906. S. S. Kemp announced that "The old original Red Boiling Springs is receiving guests daily." He continued that the water there was "making cures of liver, stomach, kidney and bladder troubles, as [it] has been doing for over seventy-five years.

June 15, 1906. Squire Obediah Donoho announced that "Donoho's new hotel is now open at Red Boiling Springs and is the best equipped and furnished house in the place." Donoho continued that "all who want to go to Red Boiling Springs will make no mistake stopping at this hotel, for we have Red Boiling and Black Sulphur that the world cannot beat." He pointed that he could offer guests "all kinds of games and a large amusement hall in connection with [the] hotel for dancing and other amusements."

Donoho added that representatives would meet "all parties" coming to Red Boiling Springs as they disembarked from the various trains and bring them to the hotel. Hotel rates were $1 or $1.50 per day. That was about $35 to $52.50 per day in today's currency.

June 29, 1906. Sarah Willis Sloan, 61, of Linden, Tennessee died at Nashville. She had been in ill health for several years and when her condition grew worse, she travelled to Red Boiling Springs hoping the waters there would cure her. However, the fresh air and mineral waters did not help her. Her doctor realized that she was terminal and advised her to return home.

Sloan made it as far as her sister's home in Nashville at 1214 Second Avenue South but was too ill to go further. She remained at her sister's residence until death overtook her. Sarah Sloan was the spouse of James L. Sloan.

James L. Sloan, who was 65, was also very ill. He went to Red Boiling Springs in search of improving his health, but with no good effect. Sloan returned to Nashville on August 13 and underwent an operation. For the first few days after the operation Sloan exhibited improvement, but he took a sudden turn for the worse and lingered until August 26, when he died.

Sloan was a past Grand Master of the Masonic Order in Tennessee.

June 30, 1906. Chief of the Improved Order of the Red Men in Nashville, Charles B. Brooks, went to Red Boiling Springs to recover his health. He improved quickly.

August 3, 1906. Red Boiling Springs remained a prime location for weddings. Ruth Ellen Turner of Gamaliel, Kentucky, and Edward S. Schubert were wed there. Schubert was a conductor for the Nashville and Decatur division of the Louisville & Nashville Railroad.

August 14, 1906. Robert Donald Goodlett, Jr. was on his way from Nashville to Red Boiling Springs for a vacation. Goodlettsville, Tennessee was named for his uncle, Adam Gibb Goodlett. On August 17, Hammonds Goodlett joined his brother Robert Donald Goodlett, Jr. at the resort.

August 22, 1906. Physicians continued to prescribe the waters and restful quiet of Red Boiling Springs for their patients. For example, the Secretary of the Tennessee State Railroad Commission, Charles H. Love, suffered from heart disease. His doctors advised him to "take a rest" for a month at Red Boiling Springs. Love followed their advice and took a leave of absence until late September.

September 27, 1906. Edna Vance of Hartsville, Tennessee, and C. C. Hayes, a traveling salesman from Louisville, Kentucky were wed at Red Boiling Springs. The marriage was a surprise, especially to the bride's father, Jordan Carr Vance. He said he had no idea that the couple had nuptials planned.

October 14, 1906. Samuel Henry of Guntersville, Alabama died in a Nashville hospital. He had been in failing health for a considerable time and he had gone to Red Boiling Springs in hopes of finding a recovery. Finding no relief from the waters at Red Boiling Springs, Henry travelled to Nashville to consult with a doctor. However, before the physician could do him any good, Henry "suddenly became worse, and sank rapidly until the end."

June 13, 1907. Robert McEwen "knew the hotel business from start to finish. He had served as chief clerk at Nashville's world-famous Maxwell House Hotel (Maxwell House coffee is named for it) for 19 years. Before then, he had managed the resort at Fernvale Springs in Fairview, Tennessee for 10 years, and Blount Springs near Brimingham, Alabama for two seasons.

McEwen was very popular at the Maxwell House, but he was lured away to replace S. S. Kemp and become the new manager of the Red Boiling Springs Hotel and resort during the summer months. McEwen was a proven commodity, and no one doubted that he would guide Red Boiling Springs to new heights.

At the end of each summer season at Red Boiling Springs, McEwen returned to the Maxwell House and resumed his duties there.

McEwen died on October 23, 1916.

July 14, 1907. Newlyweds Mr. and Mrs. J. P. Knight of Columbia, Tennessee returned home after honeymooning at Red Boiling Springs.

August 4, 1907. Joseph Franklin Carr and Selmer "Seddie" Carr were wed in the Willard Community of Trousdale County, Tennessee. She was the youngest daughter of Joseph Marshall "Dikey" Carr. After the ceremony, the newlyweds travelled to Red Boiling Springs for their honeymoon.

Also on August 4, Frank M. Davis of Nashville was at Red Boiling Springs trying to improve his health when he learned that his spouse had suffered a heart attack at La Harpe, Kansas and had died. Naturally, Davis left immediately for Kansas.

August 11, 1907. The "enormous influx" from Nashville to Tennessee's summer resorts such as Red Boiling Springs continued unabated. Some Nashvillians went to places like Atlantic City, but most remained in the Volunteer State. The reasons they gave were that they could find rest as well as comfort, and pleasure at the rural resorts. Besides that, Nashville was only a few hours away.

March 4, 1908. Manager of the Red Boiling Springs Hotel, Robert McEwen, wed Ella Mai Leneave in a grand ceremony at her home in Nashville. Both parties were mature. Ella had an adult daughter.

June 13, 1908. Hotel proprietor Mrs. F. E. Brown offered the prospective guests "hot and cold baths." She also touted the fact that she hadn't increased rates from the previous year. They remained $1 per day.

June 19, 1908. Robert and Ella McEwen threw a dance in honor of Ella's daughter, Luelle Leneave, age 14, at the Red Boiling Springs Hotel. About 20 guests attended. Some guests came from the Tennessee cities including Nashville, Lafayette, and Columbia. Others came from Birmingham, Alabama and Marlow, Oklahoma.

After the dance, the hosts served a midnight lunch. A midnight lunch is a social meal enjoyed in the middle of the night. It is less formal than a regular dinner.

Luelle would attend Nashville's Buford College that autumn.

June 21, 1908. Abraham Moore of Boyd's Creek in Barren County, Kentucky, died at Tompkinsville on his way home from Red Boiling Springs. Moore had suffered from kidney disease for many years, and he had ventured to Red Boiling Springs to "find relief." When his condition "only became worse," he decided to return home.

July 31, 1908. The clerk of the Maxwell House Hotel, Frank Davis, was spending a few weeks at the Red Boiling Springs Hotel. He was the guest of his close friend, William McEwin. Davis and McEwin had worked together at the Maxwell House for years.

Davis returned to work on August 21.

August 16, 1908. Sam Beck, an African American man who worked as a cook at the Cloyd House in Red Boiling Spring, "ran amok" and caused considerable problems both there and earlier at the hotel operated by Mrs. F. E. Brown.

Beck, who allegedly had been drinking, went to Brown's hotel and started a "roughhouse" with the cooks and waiters there. Finally, Mrs. Brown's son, Ray Wallace, broke up the disturbance and demanded that Beck leave the establishment. Beck left, but soon returned and called Wallace outside.

The two men met in front of the hotel and an argument ensued. An irate Beck cursed Wallace and then pulled his pistol and pointed its barrel at the hotel manager's son. Beck pulled the trigger thrice and the gun snapped each time. Frustrated, Beck left the scene, but he returned after apparently securing another weapon. Wallace didn't come out again, so Beck opened fire on the hotel.

The hotel clerk telephoned Lafayette and informed Macon County Sheriff James Ragland of the situation. The Sheriff deputized James Bennett, a Nashville resident named Smitherman, and others to go to Brown's hotel and arrest Beck.

When the deputies arrived, they discovered that Beck had departed. The posse then went to Cloyd Place where they found Beck. Beck was in no mood to surrender, and a gun battle broke out. Between 25 and 30 shots rang out before Beck escaped from his pursuers. No one suffered serious injury, but a bullet did "graze" Smitherman's ankle.

Beginning the next day, Sheriff Ragland led a manhunt for Beck, who was from Carthage, but did not find and apprehend the fugitive immediately.

March 23, 1909. It is not a good idea to try to hide out at a world-famous resort. Private Detective C. A. Estes had been on the trail of Nashville's M. N. Whittaker for some time. The persistent detective finally located the fugitive at Red Boiling Springs and arrested him. Whittaker was charged with stealing about $400 from the Stubler Computing Scale Company. Whittaker denied any wrongdoing and made bail.

April 11, 1909. There was an alleged rare mineral specimen found in Red Boiling Springs. Vacationing at the resort a Nashville newspaperman found the unusual stone. Uncertain of what it was, the reporter took the item to Nashville and let a noted geologist see it. The object puzzled the geologist. He said, "In all my experience I have never a specimen that resembled this one."

The geologist inquired of the reporter, "Tell me something about where you found it."

The man that found the item was hazy about the rock formations around the resort, but he did describe "the earth, air, and sky around Red Boiling Springs." The description offered the geologist no clue as to what the piece of material was. Yet, the geologist was so enamored with the Red Boiling Springs mystery stone that he moved away some lesser rocks and gave the strange object a place of honor among his collection.

Still stumped, the newspaperman suggested that they take the rare specimen to General Gates P. Thurston and let him see it. Thurston was knowledgeable in such matters. In fact, he had authored books about ancient artifacts. On their way to see Thurston the two men decided that the rare find was too precious to be kept in a private collection and as soon as they learned what it was exactly, they would donate it to the Tennessee Historical Society.

The strange little piece puzzled Thurston as much as it had the other two men. As the three men talked, the geologist formed the opinion that the item might be some heretofore never seen variety of soapstone. He opened his pocketknife and gently scraped the outside of the mystery stone. A sticky brown substance adhered to the knife blade. Almost by reflex, the geologist put the blade to his mouth and tasted the substance. Surprised, he exclaimed, "Why, it is sweet!"

At that point, the newspaperman knew what the mystery stone was. He took the specimen and "calmly bit off the corner" of his great geological discovery. His belief confirmed, the embarrassed newspaperman informed the two experts that the mystery stone was actually a piece of maple sugar that his wife had intended to give to another guest at the hotel in a box of candy, but she had misplaced it.

June 20, 1909. It was time for the Red Boiling Springs Hotel to be remodeled and its furniture replaced. The hotel manager went to Nashville and made a "handsome offer" to the proprietor of Clover Leaf Furniture. Clover Leaf accepted the offer, and the company provided enough furniture to make the hotel "look like new."

August 2, 1909. Minerva Walker, age 62, of Bass, Alabama died at Red Boiling Springs. Her spouse, Jacob Tally Walker, was one of northern Alabama's richest citizens. She had been in "feeble health" for several months and had traveled to Red Boiling Springs hoping to recapture her health.

September 15, 1909. Some 150 to 200 Macon County residents were expected to attend the Tennessee State Fair and the two big watering holes of Macon County, Epperson Springs and Red Boiling Springs were to have exhibits "that would be a credit to any county in the state."

September 24, 1909. There were rumors that a group of Nashville entrepreneurs intended to build a new hotel at Red Boiling Springs, but details remained sketchy.

July 11, 1910. Several members of the Nashville police force were on vacation at Red Boiling Springs. A Sergeant named Meadows, and Patrolmen John Van Tien and Robert McKinstry were already at the resort, and Detective Charles R. Woosley joined them on July 18. In a letter, Van Tien said he and the other officers were enjoying themselves drinking mineral water and eating "hominy" and "gravy."

September 9, 1910. Lucile Marion Leneave, age 16, wed James Wright Thompson of Birmingham, Alabama. The wedding took place at the Red Boiling Springs Hotel operated by her mother Ella McEwen and stepfather, Robert McEwen. The groom was the son of Colonel N. F. Thompson, one of Birmingham's pioneer real estate dealers.

The marriage unraveled quickly and on December 17 the child bride filed for divorce in the Davidson County Circuit Court. The stated grounds for divorce were "cruel and inhuman treatment, abandonment and failure to provide."

Lucile stated that she had intended to return to Buford College but "she was so strongly importuned by [Thompson] to marry him that she finally consented to do so and that they were hurriedly married at Red Boiling Springs by a justice of the peace."

She continued that on September 19 her husband brought her to Nashville, and they registered at the Hermitage Hotel where she and Thompson lived "very unhappily for about two weeks." Lucile stated that during this time Thompson accused her of having "improper relations" with other men. She also quoted her husband as saying that he "did not consider that they were legally married, but that they were merely on a lark."

But there was more. Lucile alleged that Thompson was a "heavy drinker" and a drug abuser. She said that on several occasions he took articles of her clothing and pawned them, "appropriating the proceeds thereof for drink and drugs to satisfy his unnatural appetites."

Lucile stated that Thompson had violent outbursts and that he had threatened to commit suicide. She said that he had become so violent once that she had to call in someone to take a pistol away from him. The incident made her nervous and desperate. She, "being actually in fear of her life," fled from her hotel room and escaped to her mother's house in Nashville.

Thompson had then gone to where Lucile was staying and told her that "he did not want to live with her and that he did not care for her." Soon thereafter, Thompson went to New York City.

May 19, 1911. Colonel John Stubblefield of the Internal Revenue Service was at Red Boiling Springs, but taxes weren't on his mind. He was there on vacation.

June 24, 1911. Dr. William Henry Franklin Glasgow, age 49, of Lebanon, Tennessee died heart failure. He had been in declining health for some time, and he gone to Red Boiling Springs shortly before his death in hopes of regaining his vigor.

July 21, 1911. The renowned Presbyterian minister, Reverend George Washington Shelton, was on vacation at Red Boiling Springs. He pastored the First Presbyterian Church of Clarksville, Tennessee (1896-1899); First Presbyterian Church of Jackson, Tennessee (1899-1901); Russell Street Presbyterian Church of Nashville (1901-1910); and the Second Presbyterian Church of Pittsburgh (1910-1936).

September 22, 1911. Some of the marriages conducted at Red Boiling Springs didn't end happily. Olivia Upham filed for divorce in Nashville. She said her husband made "no attempt" to provide for her and their little daughter. The couple wed at Red Boiling Springs in 1908 when she was only 15.

October 26, 1911. Ethel Johnson and Dr. J. Bedford Hix, both of Jackson County's Flynn's Lick community, were married. The nuptials took place quietly at the home of the bride's father with a few friends and family present. After the ceremony, the couple went to Red Boiling Springs for their honeymoon.

February 15, 1912. A fire of unknown origin destroyed the Dedman Hotel owned by the Red Boiling Springs Water Company. The blaze spread so rapidly that virtually nothing was saved. The loss was estimated at $14,000 and Red Boiling Spring Hotel manager, B. Kirk Rankin said the hotel's insurance policy was for only $7,000.

June 26, 1912. In an event of "social interest" in Nashville, Elizabeth Laurence McQuiddy and Samuel Wilson Shacklett wed. The lavish ceremony took place at the home of the bride's parents on Gallatin Pike. On the morning after the wedding, the couple went to Red Boiling Springs for their honeymoon.

September 13, 1912. The proprietors of the hotels at Red Boiling Springs felt they were victims of discrimination by the Louisville & Nashville and the Nashville, Chattanooga & St. Louis Railroad companies. In a brief filed before the Examiner of the

Interstate Commerce Commission, hotel owners claimed that the railroads had failed to sell through tickets outside of Tennessee to locations nearest to Red Boiling Springs. Specifically, the brief alleged that those going to Red Boiling Springs had to go to Nashville, rebuy their tickets and recheck their bags. The brief also stated that those going to Red Boiling Springs could not purchase round-trip tickets as those going to northern resorts could.

The attorney for the Louisville & Nashville Railroad denied the charge of discrimination. The lawyer stated that the reason for not selling through tickets via the Tennessee Central Railroad was that there was a better and more direct route on the Louisville & Nashville Railroad to Westmoreland and then by hack to Red Boiling Springs.

The Nashville, Chattanooga & St. Louis Railroad attorney also denied that it had practiced discrimination. Acknowledging that it was a complicated case, the examiner agreed to accept briefs until November 5.

March 30, 1913. There had been "considerable improvement" made to the Donoho Hotel. Tennessee D. "Tenny" Chitwood had "installed an acetylene lighting plant and turned night into day." She was also "bent on conforming to the requirements of [Tennessee's] sanitary hotel law.

Acetylene (carbide) lamps burned calcium carbide pellets and were used to light buildings and for other purposes. They were used extensively in rural areas that didn't have electric power in the first halve of the 20th century.

April 20, 1913. One of the hotels in Red Boiling Springs was for sale or rent. The hotel offered prospective buyers 35 unfurnished rooms, a two-acre garden, and red and black sulfur water. The Murray-Dibrell Shoe Company in Nashville was handling the transaction.

June 7, 1913. Pauline Stewart and Henry Rush Hampton of Cowan wed in a lavish affair. More than 50 people attended the wedding. Immediately after becoming united in marriage, they departed on the 130-mile trip to Red Boiling Springs for their honeymoon.

June 22, 1913. Billing his hotel as "the health resort of the South," W. H. Kirkpatrick, the manager of the newly christened Nashville House in Red Boiling Springs, advised vacationers, "Better Be Safe than Sorry. Stop at the Nashville House near the original springs. Cuisine the best; nights always cool; everything new for 1913, except the water.

July 11, 1913. Horace Greeley "H. G." Hill returned from Red Boiling Springs where he had been recuperating. He founded the first H. G. Hill Food Store in 1895, and more than 100 stores followed. The company remains in business today.

July 20, 1913. W. H. Kirkpatrick threw a grand barbecue for the guests of Nashville House at Red Boiling Springs. The hotel was doing good business and had received about 30 new guests over the past week. They came from across Tennessee and from such other places as Louisville; Mooresville, Alabama; Decatur, Alabama, and New Orleans.

April 19, 1914. Bug Shoulders was in Nashville purchasing supplies for the new Palace Hotel which he would manage at Red Boiling Springs. Shoulders planned to make the Palace one of the country's best hotels. He bought nothing but the "highest grade fancy groceries and table luxuries."

June 18, 1914. Bug Shoulders declared that his "A brand new structure with every convenience for the comfort of summer guests" was open. He continued, "Get away from the city's dirt and heat and visit a cool, pleasant resort with moderate prices." Daily room rates were $2 and up. One could get to the Palace by taking the Tennessee Central Railroad to Carthage and then taking a car to Red Boiling Springs. Or one could depart Nashville via boat as described in Chapter 3.

The historical marker at the Palace states that Charles Bancroft McClellan built the three-story, 185 room wooden structure on the site of the old Webb (later Dedman) hotel in 1912.

June 28, 1914. Tennessee established the Pure Food Department under the State Department of Health and began sending inspectors to hotels and other places to check on sanitary conditions. In late June, a traveling salesman named W. R. Trigg commented on the conditions at Red Boiling Springs. Trigg said he spent the first 12 days of June there and "noticed that the sanitary conditions were just the same as four years" before. Trigg continued that the state Hotel Inspector sent one of his "best men," Dr. Draper, to the resort. Draper received praise for "playing no favorites." Trigg finished by saying that what Draper "accomplished is a credit to the hotel inspection and pure food department."

August 21, 1914. One of the "most delightful" events of the season took place at the "handsome new Palace Hotel." There was a reception and a dance with some 400 guests present. The guests came from across Tennessee, Kentucky, and from such diverse places as Birmingham, Alabama and Oklahoma City, Oklahoma.

The entire lower floor of the hotel was decorated with lovely yellow flowers and Jennie Outlaw and Joe Reid served grape punch from tables set up in the lobby. Some 75 couples took part in a "grand march" and a 10-piece orchestra furnished the music. For the guests not dancing, there were contests that included nice prizes.

September 28, 1914. W. H. Gray, the State Secretary of the Supreme Council of the Royal Arcanum was taking a vacation of two weeks at Red Boiling Springs. The Royal Arcanum was a fraternal organization founded in 1877. Today, it is little more than an insurance company. It is currently not licensed to do business in Tennessee.

October 2, 1914. At 4:40 p.m., Reverend J. L. Goodnight, age 68, of Hopkinsville, Kentucky died at the Palace Hotel. Goodnight was the clerk and treasurer of the Cumberland Presbyterian Church. Suffering from heart disease, dropsy, and Bright's Disease, Goodnight and his spouse came to Red Boiling Springs on September 17, "it being hoped that he would be benefitted by the water." Early on, "it was supposed that his condition was improving." However, a few days later he had a relapse. Then, at dinner on October 1, Goodnight became distressed and although he received treatment from doctors H. C. Hesson and Frank H. Jenkins, his condition never improved and he died the next afternoon.

November 10, 1914. Alec Pedigo and Donna Clark, both of Red Boiling Springs, were wed there. Pedigo was a successful farmer and Clark was the daughter of Red Boiling Springs merchant, R. R. Clark.

February 20, 1915. Rufus Lashlee, age 75, of Big Sandy, Tennessee died at Red Boiling Springs. A "pioneer merchant" at Big Sandy, Lashlee had been in failing health for two years. He left for Red Boiling Springs on February 19, desperately hoping to regain his former vigor, but he died within hours of reaching the resort.

May 13, 1915. Zachariah Wheat Cloyd of Cloyd Place at Red Boiling Springs was looking for a new cook. He didn't care if his new cook was male or female, but he wanted to hire a white person. He didn't say why he wanted a white cook, but it was interesting because he had employed many African Americans in the past.

June 21, 1915. Myrtle Jordan, age 23, of Nashville died at Hartsville at about 10 p.m. She suffered from Bright's disease and her husband had taken her to Red Boiling Springs in hopes that she would improve. They were on their way home when she perished.

July 4, 1915. The Bradford furniture company in Nashville announced that it had "completely furnished" a large hotel in Red Boiling Springs.

July 14, 1915. Zachariah Cloyd, the proprietor of Cloyd Place offered rooms at $8.75 weekly. He advised vacationers from Nashville to purchase a "rail ticket to Carthage or Hartsville" and then hire a car to Red Boiling Springs. He told pleasure seekers to "look for" drivers Jack Knight, H. J. Harley, or William Moss. Cloyd added that there were also "independent" drivers that would bring guests to the resort.

August 8, 1915. Ira C. Harmon was a traveling salesman from Nashville. After several years of marriage, he and his spouse went to Red Boiling Springs and finally took their honeymoon. Harmon made several observations about the resort:

"Most people who come here motor through. I 'Forded' it, and I am glad to say that while the roads are a little rough, we found them much better than we expected that they would be. We made the trip through in about six and one-half hours, coming by way of Gallatin, Hartsville, and Lafayette, and had very little trouble.

Of Red Boiling Springs, he said, "This is a grand old place — three hotels and a number of private boarding houses.

"Everyone here seems to be convalescing. The ladies knit, crochet, and sew. And some of them are pretty good bowlers. The men read, smoke, and bowl — and eat.

I would advise anyone needing rest or a good liver and kidney water to come here."

August 27, 1915. At about 2 a.m. It was discovered that the Donoho Hotel was on fire. The blaze which "completely destroyed" the building was believed to have been caused by "defective flue in the kitchen. A flue is a pipe or opening in a chimney used for allowing smoke to escape a building.

No one was injured, but a few of the guests barely escaped the flames. Several guests, still in their nightclothes, got to the ground from the upper rooms by climbing down ropes. One man made it to safety by climbing out of his window onto a tree limb and climbing down to the ground. Two women were carried from the hotel by self-appointed rescuers.

The estimated damage to the three-story building was $8,000 and the owners, Brade and Tennie Chitwood, had no insurance.

The hotel owners "secured another hotel," where they received their patrons during the remainder of the season.

A new Donoho Hotel was soon erected.

September 13, 1915. Harry W. Smith died at his home in Glasgow, Kentucky. He had just returned from Red Boiling Springs where he had gone to recoup his health. Upon his return, he was feeling better, and he was out and about during the day on September 11. However, that evening, he had a "serious attack" from which he never recovered.

May 6, 1916. The manager of the Palace Hotel in Red Boiling Springs, Henry Counts, declared that the establishment was open for the season. He said the Palace offered a new amusement hall and a free garage. Counts said guests could pay by the day or by the week.

July 12, 1916. It had been raining at Red Boiling Springs for four consecutive days and a Palace Hotel guest, Judge Milligan of Boiling Green, Kentucky grew very bored. Milligan decided to have some fun with the endless downpour. The judge presented a petition requesting an injunction against hotel proprietor Henry Counts restraining him from allowing any more rain. Another hotel guest, Chancellor Newman granted the injunction, but the rain did not stop. The hotel guests then demanded the arrest of Counts for contempt of court, but even that did not lessen the deluge.

As a travelling salesman looked out his window at the rain, he thought "Why not have a celebration?" There was no celebration he could think of better than Christmas. It didn't matter if it was July, a Christmas celebration would kill some time on a rainy day. The salesman appointed a committee to acquire a Christmas Tree and a woman named McGregor led a group in decorating the tree. They adorned it with popcorn, peanuts, apples, and instead of snow, flour.

At 8 p.m. on July 12, the Christmas tree was unveiled, and gag gifts were passed about. While the Christmas in July program didn't bring the rain to an end, it did make the situation a little more bearable.

July 29, 1916. Cloyd Place had been "taken over" by a new corporation. The group called the Red Boiling Springs Company was headed by Joseph H. Peter who was originally from Louisville, Kentucky. The company was expending a great deal of its $50,000 [more than $1.4 million in today's currency] in capital stock to improve the resort.

According to reports, "new life [was] to be infused" into the place as it had been "thoroughly overhauled and remodeled." The new management said the hotel was now "first-class in all respects." It had added electric lighting, and had installed a "perfect" sewer system, and private waterworks providing all rooms with hot and cold running water. Additionally, Cloyd Place had a new heating system that would mean that it would no longer merely be a summer resort but would be an "all-the-year-round" place and would receive guests in the winter, as well as in the other seasons of the year.

Cloyd Place also offered excellent cuisine and its cooks could provide meals for those on "special diets." Moreover, the hotel had a medical doctor and an osteopath on staff.

Pundits held that "this modern hotel fills a long-felt want at Red Boiling Springs," and with the improved facilities, and "excellent transportation services," Cloyd Place would "achieve still greater success."

August 6, 1916. Tennessee Food and Drug Commissioner Harry L. Eskew issued his July report on inspections of hotels and restaurants. The following hotels and boarding houses in Red Boiling Springs received "correction" notices: Cloyd Place,

Donoho Hotel, Miller House, New Central Hotel (sometimes called New Central Motel), and Williams Hotel.

August 5, 1916. A group of guests at the Donoho Hotel formed the "Jollity Club." The purpose of the club was to have fun. There were 32 charter members of the club, and they represented Tennessee, Kentucky, and Alabama. The "chief amusements" enjoyed by members of the club included motoring, dancing, bowling, walking, and drinking water. The Jollity Club agreed to meet at the Donoho Hotel every year on the first Saturday in August.

August 8, 1916. William B. Alley, a sportswriter for the *Montgomery Advertiser* of Alabama wed in Nashville to a woman from Georgia. Immediately after the wedding, the happy couple traveled to Red Boiling Springs for their honeymoon.

September 10, 1916. In his August inspection, Tennessee Food and Drug Commissioner Harry L. Eskew found that the Palace Hotel was in excellent condition. He issued the hotel the highest rating possible – a "Certificate of Good Character."

September 11, 1916. The management of the Cloyd Place declared that it offered "all the comforts of a modern hotel – far from the city's noise and vexations." Hotel management continued that a stay there would "accomplish wonders for the tired or diseased body. Hotel accommodations satisfy the most exacting." But that wasn't all. The management stated that "Two weeks of perfect comfort and rest, with the healing powers of our wonderful waters will make you a new person. September is a delightful time to be at Red Boiling Springs. The modern, comfortable, convenient hotel of Red Boiling Springs will bring you health and pleasure."

May 24, 1917. Henry Counts announced that the Palace Hotel was open for the season. He declared, "This is a new hotel at the old springs." He added, "We have the famous Little Red" water.

July 28, 1917. There was a meeting at the dancing pavilion of the Donoho Hotel. The purpose of the meeting was to promote the work of the American Red Cross in Macon County. The work of the Red Cross had become more important since April 1917, when the United States entered World War I.

People from across the state attended the meeting. The main speaker at the event was former Tennessee State Senator and State Board of Control Member, Lewis "Luke" Pope. Pope was a future candidate for Governor, but he wasn't elected.

Pope "stressed patriotism, loyalty to President Wilson, [the precarious] food supply and [its] conservation, and forgetfulness of self, no matter the cost."

The event was marked by the raising of "Old Glory" in front of the hotel.

July 31, 1917. Visitors from Nashville remained the life's blood of the Red Boiling Springs resort. There were at least 135 Nashvillians staying at either Cloyd Place, the Donoho, or the Palace.

August 17, 1917. There was a "Tacky Party" held at the dancing pavilion of the Donoho Hotel for the benefit of the American Red Cross. It was open to everyone and guests of the Donoho Hotel, the Palace Hotel, and Cloyd Place attended and others attended. About 30 people dressed in the wackiest and most garish customs that they could think up and another 300 people enjoyed the party. The event raised $53 for the Red Cross and was declared a success.

August 26, 1917. Harry L. Eskew ordered the prosecution of two hotel operators at Red Boiling Springs for violations of the "sanitary hotel law." Martha Gaines and Hudson Hotel operator, R. M. Hudson, were cited because "their toilets were not of a sanitary design and were not property screened and disinfected." Eskew was cracking down on violators, and he had the power to shut down hotels, but the offenses he ticketed Gaines and

Hudson for didn't rise to that level. They each received $10 fines and had to pay court costs.

Eskew issued correction notices to Cloyd Place, the Palace Hotel, and the B. O. Hagan House.

The Donoho Hotel and the Missouri House received Certificates of Good Character.

September 18, 1917. There was an outbreak of smallpox in Red Boiling Springs. Several cases had appeared at the hotel suddenly. The speculation was that the disease was introduced by members of the Mighty Haag Circus when the show played there at the beginning of September. A local woman had been hired to do laundry for some members of the troupe. They told her that they had suffered from smallpox sometime before but that they had recovered. Convinced that there was no danger, she continued with her work.

About 10 days later the washerwoman came down with smallpox. It spread to her family members and then to others. Despite reassurances from the resort doctors that the disease was in "light form" and "not serious," several guests "became frightened," checked out, and returned home.

May 23, 1918. The Central Hotel at Red Boiling Springs was sold at auction for approximately $10,000. The syndicate purchasing the hotel consisted mostly of local investors. The sale included all the buildings, mineral wells, and several acres of land formerly owned by J. R. Smith. The sale drew such attention that despite heavy rain, there was a large crowd of bidders and spectators.

The new owners expected to assume operation of the hotel on June 1. They were chomping at the bit to get started. There were already many guests at the various hotels and observers expected "the biggest season Red Boiling Springs has ever known."

June 6, 1918. J. B. Freeman, O. G. Davis, Frank P. Dixon, O. R. York, and H. C. Howser formed the Red Boiling Hotel Company. The capital stock investment was $15,000 (almost $300,000 today).

July 2, 1918. F. N. Boensch Jr., age 49, died at his home in Joelton, Tennessee. He had travelled to Red Boiling Springs "in search of rest and restoration to his accustomed health." On the return trip home, he suffered a "sudden sinking spell" and "grew rapidly worse" before passing away.

July 4, 1918. The women of the Red Boiling Springs chapter of the American Red Cross held a large Fourth of July celebration. Orators demanded that citizens make sacrifices to ensure victory in the "Great War." They also praised the work of the American Red Cross.

After the speeches concluded, the women auctioned off items donated by chapter members. A cake baked by the mother of a soldier fighting at the front was "sold and resold" until it brought $45. But the prize of the auction was "a Rhode Island Red pullet dressed as Uncle Sam. The bird netted $175. In all, the auction raised $400 with the full amount going to the local Red Cross chapter.

July 21, 1918. The guests of the Palace Hotel met at the pavilion there and celebrated recent Allied victories. The event included music and patriotic speeches. Enthusiasm grew to the point that a fund was raised to adopt French and Belgian children orphaned by the war. The participants raised $146 for that purpose and passed it on to the Woman's Committee of the Macon County Council of Defense. The $146 was enough to provide for four orphans for one year.

As soon as the orphans' names were made known, they were framed and hung in the hall of the Palace Hotel.

August 20, 1918. There was a patriotic gathering on the front lawn of the Donoho Hotel. About 300 guests from the Donoho Hotel, Palace Hotel, and Cloyd Place attended. Participants from Tennessee, Kentucky, and Alabama recited poems and sang songs. Then there was an auction of boxed candles, homemade cakes, and flour. The auction raised $117.50. Additionally, an offering raised $35.11 bringing the total to $152.61. The money was turned over to Dr. H. C. Hesson, Treasurer of the Macon County Red Cross unit.

September 4, 1919. Four local men: Herman Desmond Shoulders, his brother Roey Dewey Shoulders, and Pony Oscar Witcher and *his* brother, Ellis Timberlake Witcher purchased a tract of land in the center of Red Boiling Springs. They intended to build a large, 150 room hotel on the property. The men expected to have the hotel built and open by the 1920 vacation season. The men promised that their hotel would have "furnace heat so that the sick will have accommodations" year-round.

July 8, 1920. Joseph H. Peter encouraged pleasure seekers to "spend your vacation a Cloyd Place." The hotel offered "moderate rates, high, beautiful location; six kinds of water." It offered something for the infirmed as well. Peter said, "These waters have been known for many years for their health-giving properties."

August 1, 1920. Harry L. Eskew was on vacation at Red Boiling Springs. Even though Eskew had issued citations to Red Boiling Springs hotels in the past, he maintained "great faith in the liquid refreshment to be obtained at the famous resort." Eskew expected that after he completed his two-week sojourn at Red Boiling Springs he would be "as keen as a razor blade."

May 13, 1921. Samuel A. Handly was buried in Nashville. He had suffered a fall while on vacation at Red Boiling Springs and had never recovered from his injuries.

June 19, 1921. Henry Counts of the Palace Hotel announced that beginning on July 2, William Green and his orchestra would serve at the hotel's house band for the remainder of the season.

May 15, 1922. Proprietor of Cloyd Place, Joseph H. Peter, age 66, died at the Protestant Hospital in Nashville. He had been suffering from anemia for at least six months.

The Protestant Hospital was incorporated on December 12, 1918, in reaction the Spanish Flu epidemic then wreaking havoc throughout the United States. In 1948, the Protestant Hospital merged with Baptist Hospital.

July 9, 1922. Mr. and Mrs. Hardy Burt of Decatur, Tennessee were the honored guests given at Red Boiling Springs celebrating their wedding anniversary.

July 31, 1922. Madame Kazaza, the "demon fortuneteller" had gone into seclusion in Nashville while she prepared for a trip to Red Boiling Springs "to rest up from the labors of her tidy little soothsaying business." Before hiding herself away, she performed "some fatiguing crystal gazing and some calculations in astronomy." The result was that she made some vague predictions about the upcoming primary elections.

Madame Kazaza returned from her stay at the resort on August 5. She said that during her stay she discerned that the springs at Red Boiling Springs were neither "red" nor "boiling." She also claimed that her election predictions were virtually perfect.

August 7, 1922. Thomas Goodall, chief stockholder, and Vice President of the Nashville Vols minor league baseball team attended a game, then he, his spouse Sarah, two of their children, and their niece departed for a vacation at Red Boiling Springs.

June 24, 1923. Dr. Royal A. Leslie of Red Boiling Springs reported that a 265-gallon tank he had purchased from the Old Hickory gunpowder plant of Nashville had exploded. After the explosion, Leslie said he found about three pounds of gun cotton inside the tank. The explosion marked the third such explosion of a tank coming from the plant in a week. One of the explosions killed a Nashville man.

The Old Hickory gunpowder plant was built and operated by the DuPont Corporation. During World War I the factory produced 750,000 pounds of gunpowder a day.

Oddly, there was another explosion at the Leslie home 14 years later. It had no relation to the first one. See Chapter 9.

July 19, 1923. At about 2 a.m. Joseph M. Glick, age 55, of 943 Jefferson Street in Nashville died at Red Boiling Springs. His body was returned to Nashville and he was buried on July 20.

July 31, 1923. State Hotel Inspector Sam I. Bolton completed his inspections of the hotels in Red Boiling Springs and approved them all. Bolton had been anxious to finish his inspections before "the influx of visitors began in August and September."

August 17, 1923. Chief Detective of the Nashville Police Department, Robert Sidebottom, returned to work after two weeks of pleasure at Red Boiling Springs.

October 28, 1923. Ernest Shoemake of Carthage took over the operation of the Graystone Hotel in Dickson. Shoemake had previously managed the Palace Hotel in Red Boiling Springs.

February 9, 1924. Ellis Witcher, the former manager of Cloyd Place was building a hotel on the property he purchased from R. R. Clark. This would be the second "modern" hotel built in Red Boiling Springs in the past two years. The Moss Hotel was the other one.

February 14, 1924. Henry Counts of the Palace Hotel had been seriously ill, but he was improving. By early March, Counts felt well enough to have some necessary dental work done.

March 6, 1924. The roads were improving and some 13 travelling salesmen were registered at the Palace Hotel. One of the salesmen came from Fort Worth, Texas.

March 8, 1924. The Arlington Hotel under the management of "Uncle Tom" McClellan and Dr. T. J. Meador was undergoing "reconstruction." An addition was being built onto the hotel to accommodate the influx of guests expected to arrive that summer. Beyond the additional rooms, McClellan and Meador installed "entirely new equipment."

June 15, 1924. The 171-room Palace Hotel was open for the season. The hotel had a "known reputation for sanitation, service and reasonable rates."

June 10, 1925. Many people continued to make the pilgrimage to Red Boiling Springs in hopes of restoring their health. Sadly, some of them died before reaching the secluded resort. A case in point was Jeff L. Stafford. Stafford, age 70, owned and operated the Newman Hotel in Oklahoma City, Oklahoma. He had suffered a bout of gallstones and he decided to make the 750 mile trip to Red Boiling Springs to recuperate. On the way to the resort, Stafford stopped at his brother's residence in Nashville where he died suddenly a few days later.

July 12,1925. Red Boiling Springs continued to boom every vacation season. Between the middle of June and the middle of September, the resort played host to thousands of visitors looking for health giving water and the various entertainments the resort offered.

Red Boiling Springs offered visitors any one of six major hotels (Arlington, Cloyd Place, Donoho, Moss, Palace, and Red Boiling Springs). Besides the large hotels, there were numerous smaller hotels and boarding houses available to accommodate the overflow of visitors. There were always 900 or so vacationers at the resort at any given time, and the total for the season was well into the thousands.

Visitors came from all over. In 1924, the six major hotels hosted more than 9,000 guests from 27 different states. The boarding houses took in thousands of others. Most of the vacationers came from Tennessee, with Kentucky and Alabama being the next highest in number of guests staying there. The number of visitors to the community was staggering when one considers that during that time the town's population was 500 or less.

July 19, 1925. A man named Arch Bishop was the General Sales Manager of Nashville's Standard Candy Company. He was on vacation at Red Boiling Springs. The company had manufactured Goo-Goo Clusters since 1912 and it became one of Tennessee's most recognizable brands of sweets. Today, Goo-Goo Clusters have the distinction of being Nashville's "official" candy.

July 30, 1925. A typical breakfast at the Donoho Hotel consisted of bacon and eggs, fried chicken, honey, all the biscuits one could eat, and coffee.

May 29, 1926. The Palace Hotel held a dance to open the vacation season. A "special orchestra" led by Nashville radio personality Jimmy Jackson provided music for the Saturday evening event.

June 13, 1926. Red Boiling Springs remained a very coveted honeymoon destination. Muriel Robinson and Edward Carl Fos Jr. were married in Nashville and they departed for Red Boiling Springs immediately after the ceremony concluded.

June 15, 1926. The Upper Cumberland Medical Society opened its thirty-second annual conference at Red Boiling Springs. Hundreds of doctors, many coming by personal automobile, attended and more than forty physicians presented papers. Some of the more interesting topics covered included "The Results of Radium Treatment Fibroid Tumors" and "Surgery Under Local Anesthesia."

Macon County doctors in attendance included F. B. Clark, H. C. Hesson, W. H. Counts, and S. H. Chitwood. The keynote address was delivered by outgoing society President, Dr. L. H. Beasley of Dixon Springs. His topic was "What a Physician Should Stand for in His Community."

So many doctors attended that there wasn't a single hotel that could hold them all. They spread out among the Arlington, Cloyd Place, Donoho, Moss, and Red Boiling Springs hotels.

An indication of the importance of the conference was illustrated by the fact that four members of the Tennessee State Health Department, including State Health Commissioner Dr. E. L. Bishop, attended.

Besides the serious work of the conference, the doctors and their spouses took part in a banquet and ball on the evening June 15. Unbeknownst to the doctors at the ball, a calamity was unfolding. E. H. Collier, a Lebanon farmer and merchant, had driven a Wilson County doctor to the conference. During the ball, Collier left Red Boiling Springs without telling anyone. The next afternoon, Collier and his car were found in the Cumberland River near the ferry landing at Hartsville. A Coroner's Jury held an inquest and ruled that Collier had driven off the landing in the darkness and was a victim of accidental drowning.

The last order of business at the conference was the election of officers. Dr. Edward Clark of Clay County's Willow Grove was elected President. The only Red Boiling Springs doctor elected was Dr. F. B. Clark. He was chosen second vice president.

August 6, 1926. In the early morning hours, a fire believed to have been caused by the explosion of a gas percolator damaged the two-story, 25-room Cloyd Place and two adjoining cottages beyond repair. About 40 guests escaped the flame. No one was hurt except for a woman who suffered minor injuries when she jumped from a second story window.

The hotel was owned by a group of entrepreneurs from Tennessee and Kentucky and they promised to rebuild it.

August 24, 1926. J. T. Peeler, the past Grand Master of the Tennessee Masonic Order and a prominent attorney from Huntingdon, Tennessee, and his spouse returned from a stay of two weeks at Red Boiling Springs. He said he had recovered from a recent illness.

September 5, 1926. Jimmy Jackson was one of the "jazziest" radio announcers in the South. He was also a fine pianist. Jackson had been an important talent at Nashville radio station WDAD since it signed on in 1925.

Jackson had led the orchestra at the Palace Hotel for several months, but he gave up that position to return to the radio station for the fall season. WDAD became WLAC in 1926.

June 6, 1927. The thirty-third edition of the Upper Cumberland Medical Society conference closed. During the event, more than 50 doctors presented papers dealing with important medical developments. At the close of the Conference, Dr. F. B. Clark of Red Boiling Springs was elected society president. Additionally, the group voted to move the conference from Red Boiling Springs to Cookeville in 1928.

June 23, 1927. An educational and good roads conference for the fourth congression district opened at Red Boiling Springs. The conference ran until June 26. Former State Senator J. T. Baskerville spoke at the conference. State highway officials also addressed the gathering. Charles Peay and P.M. Estes of the Nashville Auto Club were also on the program.

Beyond the serious work at the conference, the delegates were regaled with music and other entertainments.

July 15, 1927. There was another Upper Cumberland good roads conference held at Red Boiling Springs. The counties represented included Clay, Jackson, Macon, Overton, Smith, and Trousdale. The delegates contended that more roads in the Upper Cumberland should be paved by the state because most of the area remained completely dependent upon highways for their transportation. They also adopted a resolution to be presented to the Governor and the state Highway Department calling for Highway 52 to be immediately paved.

Another order of business was the Nashville Auto Club's forming several county branches. The county clubs were affiliated with the American Automobile Association and their purpose was to promote legislation providing for better roads and other matters beneficial to motorists.

The Red Boiling Springs Good Road Committee treated the delegates to a noon day banquet.

August 18, 1927. At about 2 a.m. 19-month-old Thomas Clycon Rutherford died of natural causes at Red Boiling Springs. His parents, Amos and Mary Rutherford took the youngster back to their home at 1219 Howard Ave. in Nashville. They next day, the child was buried in Mount Olivet Cemetery.

July 2, 1928. The Cloyd Hotel opened for the summer season. The new structure was purported to be "modern in every respect" and its owners promised reasonable rates. A selling point was the eight piece hotel orchestra under the direction of Lawrence Hopkins.

July 26, 1928. Chief Detective of the Nashville Police Department, Robert Sidebottom, stepped away from his duties for a short time and began a sojourn at Red Boiling Springs for 10 days.

September 1, 1928. There was a daylong rally at Red Boiling Springs sponsored by the Austin Peay Highway Association. About 500 members of the 6,000 member association attended. Governor Horton had agreed to attend, but later he declined. With the Governor elsewhere, State Highway Commissioner Harry S. Berry served as keynote speaker. Speakers from Red Boiling Springs speaking at the event included Charles B. McClellan and Professor C. W. Davis.

The association delegates were delighted by the information that the highway was graveled for almost its entire route from Middle to West Tennessee. Looking to maintain the association's momentum, the attendees voted to file articles of incorporation.

February 27, 1929. Charles Bancroft McClellan, age 50, died at his Red Boiling Springs home. His time of death was give variously as 6 p.m. and 9 p. m.

March 24, 1929. Henry Counts reminded the public that the famous Palace Hotel was open "the entire year – both winter and summer." He added that there had been many improvements to the hotel including "steam heat, hot and cold running water, baths, etc." Counts was proud that his hotel offered "good homecooked meals, prompt and courteous service," and reasonable rates.

June 4, 1929. The thirty-fifth annual meeting of the Upper Cumberland Medical Society opened at Red Boiling Springs. The society was founded in 1894 with seven members. Five of those charter members attended the 1929 meetings. As it did every year, the event featured many entertainments as well as the presentation of several scholarly papers. A dinner was given for the doctors at 6 p. m. on June 4. The meeting wound up on June 5.

June 8, 1929. The Palace Hotel hosted its first dance of the summer season. The Saturday night affair took place at the hotel's dance pavilion and music was provide by the Forrest Sander orchestra of Nashville. Dances were also planned for June 15 and June 22. Beginning on June 29, the house orchestra would give daily concerts.

June 30, 1929. The Cloyd Hotel was gearing up for its Independence Day festivities. Hotel management stated the Cloyd was "modern" in every way. Beyond daily concerts, hotel staff served lunch and dinner daily and management offered to make "special arrangements" for guests desiring to hold July parties there.

August 19, 1929. The consensus was that most of Tennessee's cold water resorts were either shutting down forever, or were in steep decline. This was not the case with Red Boiling Springs. By all appearances Red Boiling Springs was gaining in popularity nationally.

February 28, 1930. The Tennessee Highway Commission completed a survey for a "modern" bridge which would replace the "old wooden bridge" in front of the Palace Hotel property.

June 7, 1930. The Palace Hotel held its first dance of the summer season. There were dances every Saturday night through June 28. After that, there were dances every night for the remainder of the season. The 8-piece Southern Colonel Orchestra provided the music.

May 31, 1931. Thousands of visitors continued to visit Red Boiling Springs annually. The mineral water, cool breezes, and pleasant climate were drawing attractions, but there were other reasons to come as well. The sick and infirmed still came to recuperate and resident physicians H. C. Hesson and F. B. Clark were available if anyone needed medical attention.

There were those that spent their days at the Palace Hotel sitting on the long, shade covered veranda and read. Others made use of the experienced masseurs and received invigorating sulfur baths and treatments. Still others partook in horseback riding, swimming boating, dancing, bowling, and taking refreshing walks.

June 6, 1931. The Palace Hotel held its opening dance of the season. Hotel management promised thinking of driving there that the roads were good and that there were no detours. The first dance of the 1931 season featured some real star power. The "Husk" O'Hare Orchestra provided the music. O'Hare's orchestra had gained "national eminence." He had a weekly radio show that originated from Chicago's LaSalle Hotel and was broadcast nationally on the NBC radio network. O'Hare received more fan mail than any other national radio celebrity. The band leader had received some 300,000 telegrams alone.

O'Hare's orchestra also played at the Palace on July 25. The house band, the Paramount Publix Orchestra led by J. W. "Jesse" Knowles, provided music for the balance of the season.

June 16, 1931. The thirty-seventh annual meeting of the Upper Cumberland Medical Society opened its two-day session at the Palace Hotel. Knoxville physician J. B. Neill delivered the President's address titled "Progress in Medicine." During the conference, some 22 doctors delivered presentations and essays covering a wide array of medical remedies. The last order of business was choosing a new President. Dr. S. E. Gaines of Sparta received that honor.

August 28, 1931. The Austin Peay Memorial Highway Association meeting opened at Red Boiling Springs. The President of the group, C. Rex Mahr of Bells, Tennessee said, "This is an important meeting to be held at one of most important health resorts in the entire South." Proof of the meeting's importance can be found in the fact that US Senator Cordell Hull and war hero Alvin C. York attended.

The meeting, attended by more than 1,000 people, began at 1:30 p.m. and music was provided by the Red Boiling Springs Quartet. But it wasn't all fun and games. Speakers rebuked the Tennessee legislature sharply for failing to provide funds for the continuation of the state highway program.

June 1, 1932. There were several "modern" hotels operating in Red Boiling Springs. Those garnering the most attention were the Cloyd, Counts, Donoho, Lincoln, Moss, and Palace. Beyond the hotels, several boarding houses continued to do brisk business, especially during the summer months .

June 4, 1932. NBC Radio personality Art Kassel performed at the season opening dance at the Palace Hotel. The well-known band leader was also renowned as a singer, song writer, and saxophonist.

June 16, 1932. Albert Henry Counts, age 52, part owner of both the Palace and Counts Hotels, died. He managed hotels in Red Boiling Springs for 18 years until his poor health forced his retirement. His son, Albert, Jr., took over the business when his father retired. At one time the senior Counts also operated a hotel in Tompkinsville, Kentucky.

Albert Henry Counts, Jr. promised that the Counts Hotel was "modern and up to date" and had a bath in every room.

June 18, 1932. The big dance that evening at the Palace Hotel was postponed until July 2. On that date, Jesse Knowles and his Paramount Publix Orchestra was expected to arrive "intact" to perform for the remainder of the summer season.

July 8, 1932. The Palace Hotel management announced that Jesse Knowles and his Paramount Publix Orchestra had arrived. That weekend, not only did the orchestra play, but guests were entertained by the Singing O'Connor Sisters, "vaudeville's favorite toe, tap, and acrobatic dancing team." The O'Connor Sisters were Canadians that toured across North America between 1910 and 1937.

July 18, 1932. Many people included a yearly visit to Red Boiling Springs as a matter of course. One annual visitor was quoted as saying that if he "had the choice between a trip to Europe and a visit to Red Boiling," he'd go to the Tennessee resort.

One great selling point for Red Boiling Springs was that its "modern and beautiful" hotels offered "accommodations at a lower rate than nearly any other first class resort."

July 24, 1932. The Donoho Hotel was famous for its hospitality. Thousands had stayed there over the years and many returned summer after summer. The hotel owner, B. W. Chitwood, was genial and had many friends. It offered hot and cold baths and telephone service.

Another selling point for the Donoho Hotel was that it was secluded even by Red Boiling Springs standards. It sat back in a shady grove and offered a long, covered veranda which added to its relaxing atmosphere. The nights were cool and pleasant and the temperature was never too hot – at least when compared to sweltering, stuffy Nashville.

The Palace Hotel was operated by Katheryne McClellan. Open year-round, it was considered "one of the finest resort hotels to be found anywhere." Built on the banks of a tributary that some considered "a small river," it offered a shady, restful place for vacationers. The large building featured 180 rooms, most of which opened onto its large veranda. More active visitors could enjoy bowling, croquet, nightly dances, a beautiful new concrete swimming pool at the entrance of the hotel grounds, and a miniature golf course. The Palace also offered new bath houses operated by skilled attendants, and a beauty parlor and barber shop, salt rubs, vapor baths, and massages. Staff served daily meals supervised by expert dietitians. The Sunday dinners were especially noteworthy.

There were several bath houses in Red Boiling Springs. Some were seasonal, others were open year-round. Many people came from around the United States just for the mineral baths. The steam heated bath houses operated in conjunction with the Palace were the most popular.

The hotel offered weekly rates based on the "American Plan." The American Plan (which some hotels still use) includes breakfast, lunch, and dinner for the length of one's stay. Generally the rates for the American Plan are higher but offer a good value for one's money, especially for those seeking added convenience.

J. J. Hill managed the Cloyd Hotel. It was a new brick building located at the "head of the fountain." The head of the fountain was at the source of the principle mineral streams.

The Cloyd stood "serenely aloof on the summit of a hill like a castle of old." Hotel management prided itself on its cuisine that was "famed for its excellence" and promised to put the comfort of its guests first. It operated on the American Plan.

Amusements enjoyed by pleasure seekers at the Cloyd included boating, dancing, hiking, horseback riding, and swimming.

The Cloyd offered four varieties of mineral water. The double and twist waters were reputed to be "especially fine for people suffering from eczema or other skin diseases."

The Moss Hotel was managed by Mrs. N. T. Smith and featured six mineral water wells and a shade covered veranda. The hotel was centrally located which provided guests ready access to all points of interest.

Mrs. W. L. Knight managed the Hotel Lincoln and Wash Patterson and Frank P. Dixon owned it. Patterson and Dixon were also Macon County governmental officials. They were accused of embezzling county funds and of arson in connection with the burning of the Macon County Courthouse in Lafayette. Neither man was convicted.

The clientele of the Hotel Lincoln was composed mostly of vacationers that returned year after year. Mrs. Knight had many years of experience in hotel management and the hotel was known for its smooth operation. There were both mineral water and freestone water on the hotel grounds. The hotel offered several varieties of entertainment including bowling.

September 17, 1932. The Palace Hotel held a "Special Season Feature Dance." The house band performed and there was a floor show.

June 4, 1933. The Palace Hotel hired an experienced person serve as manager. Fatio Dunham took over just in time for beginning of the summer season. Dunham had for the past dozen years managed the Urmey Hotel in Miami, Florida. He had previously managed the Fleetwood Hotel at Miami Beach. Dunham had also managed major hotels in New York City and Atlantic City. He had also spent 15 summers operating the Hotel Gordon in Waynesboro, North Carolina. Charles B. "Jack" McClellan, Jr. was the assistant manager at the Palace.

The Palace offered a "sensible" vacation for those that came there for health or recreation. Daily hotel rates were $3 to $4 and the Palace was on the American Plan. It also offered special rates for those paying by the week or holding parties there.

June 6, 1933. The Upper Cumberland Medical Society opened its thirty-ninth annual convention at the Palace Hotel. The hotel management threw a dance for the doctors featuring Les Stillman's Orchestra.

June 15, 1933. The Counts Hotel was open for the season. Owned by Evie Lee "Eva" Counts, and managed by Albert Henry Counts, Jr., it offered vacationers a "new, modern, fireproof" hotel at reasonable rates. It also had new furnishings throughout and running water in every room.

June 17, 1933. The Palace Hotel marked its formal opening for the summer season. The festivities began at 5 p. m. with an old-fashioned barbecue. A dance featuring the music stylings of Roy Holmes and his Kentucky Cavaliers band followed.

June 22, 1933. The annual meeting of the Cream Improvement Associations of Indiana, Kentucky, and Tennessee opened at Red Boiling Springs. Butter manufacturers were also invited to attend.

Association members held a roundtable discussion and then named a committee to draw up a code of ethics, Later, Tennessee Commissioner of Agriculture, O. E. Van Cleave, spoke at the conference, and urged the "creamery men" to "improve" dairy products.

July 7, 1933. The annual conference of the Tennessee Press Association opened at Red Boiling Springs. More than 150 reporters from across the state attended. The Chairman of the Tennessee Valley Association, Dr. Arthur E. Morgan, agreed to address the pressmen.

Association members voted unanimously to join the Southern Press Association. It was the first group of newsmen working mostly for weekly papers to unite with pressmen working for the South's big city dailies.

July 9, 1933. All the leading hotels in Red Boiling Springs were open for the season.

The management of the Cloyd Hotel was proud of its "brick architecture of the Spanish type." It also sported running water in every room and showers in 24 of them. There was a "fine" bathhouse on the premises and it was the only one in Red Boiling Springs to utilize "Double and Twist" mineral water. As did all the other hotels at Red Boiling Springs, the Cloyd offered low rates.

The cuisine at the Hotel Lincoln was growing in fame with its management claiming that hundreds of guests praised the hotel for its "perfect menu." Management also claimed that the Hotel Lincoln offered "real Southern hospitality and modern service." Most of the visitors there came from nearby towns in Tennessee and Kentucky.

The Donoho Hotel billed itself as a "Metropolitan" hotel offering 60 "cool, comfortable, rooms" at $14 per week. For years, the Donoho had been known for its "easy hospitality and general air of quiet gentility." Located in the "very center of the springs," it was convenient for those wishing to partake of the resort's many activities.

July 12, 1933. Former Nashville Chief of Police J. W. Smith, age 75, suffered a stroke within hours of arriving at Red Boiling Springs for a vacation. The stroke left him unable to speak.

August 22, 1933. W. T. Head of Springfield, Tennessee died after suffering a stroke while at Red Boiling Springs. Head had been in failing health for months, prompting him and his wife to come to Red Boiling Springs on August 18.

September 2, 1933. The Palace Hotel management announced its Labor Day weekend schedule. September 3: Big Dance; September 4: Barbecue; September 5: Big Dance.

November 30, 1933. On Thanksgiving Day, the postal employee association of the Fifth Congressional District honored the Majority Leader of the US House, Joseph W. "Jo" Byrns. It was a big event. Three bands played in the streets and in the hotels throughout the day. Byrns met with the public for an hour in the morning and delivered an address that afternoon. Then, the postal workers and Byrns enjoyed an old-fashioned Thanksgiving Dinner.

Frequent visitor to Red Boiling Springs, Secretary of State Albert Gore, Sr., was invited to the event, as were US Senators from Tennessee, Kenneth McKellar and Nathan Lynn Bachman, Tennessee Governor Hill McAlister, and Postmaster General James A. Farley.

May 6, 1934. The Palace Hotel was accepting guests, but the formal opening of the summer season was a month away. Hotel management asked the public to watch the newspapers for the exact date of the summer season opening dance.

June 6, 1934. The fortieth annual conference of the Upper Cumberland Medical Society opened at Red Boiling Springs. It ran through June 7.

June 9, 1934. The Palace Hotel celebrated its summer opening dance. Roy Holmes and his Palace Hotel Orchestra provided the dance music.

Jack McClellan had been elevated to hotel manager and he announced that daily rates would remain $3 or $4 depending upon the room taken.

July 4, 1934. The Palace Hotel held its annual Independence Day celebration. Activities included an afternoon barbecue, a "Tea Dance" from 4:30 to 6 p.m., and then an evening dance. As usual, Roy Holmes and his Palace Hotel Orchestra provided the music for the dancers.

Throughout the day, droves of automobiles crowded the highways between Nashville and Red Boiling Springs and hundreds showed up for the celebration at the Palace.

July 11, 1934. Katheryne McClellan was badly injured in an automobile accident. She spent several days in Nashville's St. Thomas Hospital, but she recovered.

January 4, 1935. Charles Robert Jenkins, age 4, died at Hartsville while being transported in an ambulance from Red Boiling Springs to a Nashville hospital. The child and his parents lived in Nashville. Little Charles suffered from colitis and his parents had brought him to Red Boiling Springs in search of a cure.

July 4, 1935. There was a huge turnout for the Independence Day festivities at Red Boiling Springs. About 2,000 visitors came to the little town that day. The opinion was that the extremely hot weather in the large cities had much to do with the large crowds coming.

August 10, 1935. A local newspaper listed nine hotels in Red Boiling Springs: Arlington, Cloyd, Counts, Farmers, Jordan House, Knight House, Lincoln, Moss, and Palace. Bowling was a popular activity at several of the hotels.

September 2, 1935. The Palace Hotel held its annual Labor Day celebration. There was a barbecue and "matinee dance" in the afternoon followed by another dance beginning at 10 p.m. Jimmie Gallagher's Orchestra provided the music and there was free admission for all hotel guests.

October 12, 1935. The early cold weather and frost damaged crops in Red Boiling Springs, but it had little effect on the hotel business there.

January 25, 1936. The shooting gallery, beer garden, and other structures at the Palace Hotel were torn away. A new tearoom was being built near Bennett Springs.

April 2, 1936. The most widespread flu epidemic in more than a decade raged across the United States. Red Boiling was not spared. Flu killed several residents there. The epidemic receded in a few weeks and the resort business was not hurt badly by it. In fact, some 14,000 people stayed in the small town of fewer than 1,000 in 1936. The hotels could not hold every visitor that summer and autumn and the overflow stayed at the 20 or so boarding houses in the area.

June 13, 1936. The Palace Hotel hosted its first official dance of the summer season. The festivities began with a dinner from 6 to 9 p.m. followed immediately by the dance. Dinner cost 75¢ per person and admission to the dance was $1 per couple.

June 17, 1936. The Upper Cumberland Medical Society concluded its forty-second convention at the Palace Hotel. Social Security was a major topic of discussion during the convention.

June 20, 1936. At 1:30 p.m. a caravan of about 170 Shriners in about 60 cars from the Al Menah Temple departed Nashville for Red Boiling Springs. The 30 piece Al Menah brass band came along to preform for the Shriners on the lawn of the Palace Hotel.

Upon arriving at the hotel, the Shriners checked in, were serenaded by the band, and had dinner. After they ate, they enjoyed a thirty-minute fireworks display. Then at 10 p.m. they entertained themselves with a six act floor show followed at 11 p.m. by a big dance.

The Shriners had reserved about 100 rooms at the Palace and most of them departed the next day after the hotel staff had provided them with breakfast and lunch.

July 21, 1936. The Palace Hotel management reminded the public that it hosted dances there every Tuesday, Thursday, Friday, and Saturday nights.

August 22, 1936. O. M. Adams, a travelling salesman for McClung Hardware Company of Knoxville died suddenly at Red Boiling Springs. His remains were returned to his hometown of Cookeville for burial.

August 29, 1936. The Palace Hotel offered an "enjoyable and reasonable vacation [featuring] famous mineral waters, mineral baths, swimming, dancing, horseback riding, famous Southern cooking."

April 12, 1937. Dr. Royal A. Leslie was a masseur and bath house operator in Red Boiling Springs. Leslie was a doctor of Mechanotherapy, and he did good business with the summer crowd that came to Red Boiling Springs for health and pleasure.

On the evening of April 12, a bomb made from unknown materials was placed under the back porch of Leslie's home. When the bomb detonated, it blew the porch to bits and severely damaged the house. The walls of the house were torn loose from the structure and the bath house, which was connected to the house, was damaged beyond repair.

None of the Leslie family was at home at the time of the bombing. Dr. Leslie was in Michigan on business, his wife was wintering in Michigan, and their daughter was away in college.

June 1, 1937. The Palace Hotel opened for the summer season.

June 18, 1937. The two-day Tennessee Press Association annual convention opened at Red Boiling Springs. After a large banquet, the newspaper men discussed items of interest to them. Rufus F. Boddie, editor of the *Sumner County News* was elected President of the association.

July 3, 1937. The celebration of the Independence Day weekend at the Palace Hotel included dances on July 3, 4 and 5, and a "big barbecue" on July 4.

July 21, 1937. Clarence L. Watts, a defense attorney in the "Scottsboro" trials in Alabama fell ill from stress and went to Red Boiling Springs to regather his health.

The Scottsboro case involved the racially charged trials of several African American youths facing the death penalty. The trials drew national attention.

September 2, 1937. William E. Sharp, age 72, a merchant from Florence, Alabama died at his home. Sharp, who had appeared to be in good health before his sudden death, had just returned from a stay of 10 days at Red Boiling Springs.

September 10, 1937. The estimate was that by the end of the season, more than 15,000 guests would vacation at Red Boiling Springs.

October 16, 1937. Not all the hotels in Red Boiling Springs were just for vacationers on short-term visits. Some offered rooms as permanent residences. On October 16, 1937, W. K. Carr died at the Arlington Hotel. Carr, who was 70, had been living at the Arlington Hotel for about seven years.

May 29, 1938. The resort at Red Boiling Springs was often used as a rest stop by motorists who were going elsewhere. It was an ideal place to gas up, get a bite to eat, clean up, and get a little rest before continuing one's journey.

July 1, 1938. The management of the Palace Hotel spared no expense to entertain vacationers. One could often see world-class musicians at the hotel. On July 1 and 2, internationally famous jazz pianist and band leader Earl "Fatha" Hines performed at the Palace. It was a hot ticket and those that didn't make early reservations couldn't get to see Hines perform.

Roy Holmes and his Orchestra played at the Palace on July 3 and 4. Holmes and his band couldn't match Earl Hines, but they were good.

If the music wasn't enough, on July 3, there was a big barbecue at the Palace.

May 18, 1939. Business leaders in Red Boiling Springs believed its future as a resort town remained bright and they were willing to invest in that future. There was even a new hotel open for business. Called the Colonial and managed by Callie Evelyn Knight, it was in the "lower part of town and had about 30 rooms with bath and other conveniences." The hotel offered "cool, shady lawns, and other places for rest, a shuffleboard, and other forms of amusement, and various other attractions."

June 10, 1939. The Palace Hotel hosted its formal opening dance of the season. Adrian McDowell's Orchestra provided the music for the dance. Then there was a dance every Saturday night during the season.

Adrian McDowell was a popular bandleader. He and his orchestra often played at Nashville's famous Wagon Wheel restaurant and dancehall.

July 29, 1939. Nashville's Effeness Club (Every Friday Night Sewing Club) opened its two-day meeting at the Donoho Hotel.

April 14, 1940. Reports were that one of the hotels at Red Boiling Springs was up for sale. The price for the unidentified hotel was $8,000, but the owner was willing to take $2,000 cash for it.

April 21, 1940. There were more hotels in tiny Red Boiling Springs than any other Tennessee town except for the Volunteer State's four largest cities: Memphis, Nashville, Chattanooga, and Knoxville. Yet, by 1940, the number that were open outside the summer season had dwindled down to one.

June 10, 1940. Members of Vanderbilt University's Alpha Chi Omega and Delta Signa Theta sororities left for a weekend of frolicking at Red Boiling Springs.

August 31, 1940. More than 25 members of the Effeness Club had departed Nashville and arrived at Red Boiling Springs for the Labor Day weekend. The group stayed at the Cloyd Hotel and relaxed by bowling, hiking, and taking part in other activities.

August 31, 1940. The Palace Hotel kicked off its Labor Day weekend with a big Saturday night dance. There were also evening dances on Sunday and Monday. Roy Holmes and his Orchestra provided the music.

July 4, 1941. The Palace Hotel sponsored a "glorious" Fourth of July weekend. Hotel management promised motorists that they could expect a "nice drive" to the "always cool" town. Festivities that weekend included music by Roy Holmes and his "excellent" band, fine food, fireworks displays on the 4th and 5th, boxing matches, swimming, and other activities. The Palace was billed as "Tennessee's bright spot resort – where the smartest vacationers go."

June 14, 1942. The Palace Hotel opened for the summer season.

October 8, 1942. At 1 p.m., the Carter Auction Company of Scottsville, Kentucky auctioned the 34-room, fully equipped Counts Hotel. The hotel had a lot going for it. The brick structure was less than a decade old and it was located on a large plot of land in the heart of Red Boiling Springs. Along with the hotel, the purchaser would get "furniture, rugs, beds and bedding, linens, silverware." Auctioneer C. M. Turner promised easy terms for the purchaser of the hotel.

June 19, 1943. The Palace Hotel opened for the summer season. Attempting to counter those that felt it was inappropriate to frolic during wartime, hotel management stated, "It's patriotic to enjoy a healthful vacation."

June 22, 1944. The management of the Palace Hotel was still trying to convince the public that it was okay for them to vacation during wartime. The hotel proprietor stated, "The Palace Hotel, Red Boiling Springs, Tennessee, is now open for your wartime vacation. We realize that everybody is busy at war work and that all are patriotic enough to work all the longer and harder just to get the world over, however, in times of stress and strain rest periods are essential, it is not deemed unpatriotic to take vacations. The restful atmosphere and quiet of the Palace with its mineral waters and baths is recommended as a tonic for tired citizens. "

June 20, 1945. The Palace Hotel was open for the season.

3. Transportation to-and-Fro

Getting to Red Boiling Springs was difficult in the early days of the 20th Century. This chapter explores efforts to make travel to Red Boiling Springs easier while keeping it pristine and at least somewhat secluded.

June 10, 1903. The Tennessee Central Railroad released its schedule and instructed those going to Red Boiling Springs to take the train to Carthage and to catch a car from there.

February 17, 1906. The passenger department of the Southern Railway was said to be "collecting data" about the numerous small summer resorts in the Nashville area. The department intended to publish "a handsome booklet" with descriptions of the resorts. The goal was "to make a strong effort to get people from all over the South" to visit the resorts around Nashville. Of course, Red Boiling Springs was one of the resort towns to be featured.

On May 17, the Southern Railway issued "several pretty folders and booklets" advertising Tennessee summer resorts. A "neat booklet" was devoted to Red Boiling Springs, the pleasurers of the resort, as well as the curative powers of the water there. The booklet included photographs of the best hotels and cottages in the town. A separate section of the booklet included the rates at the resort and the fee to take a conveyance from the railroad station to Red Boiling Springs.

July 6, 1907. The trains leaving Nashville were always full in early July. In fact, no one could remember such heavy traffic before. Southern Railway trains were especially crowded, and observers surmised it was because many of the passengers were going to the Red Boiling Springs resort which had just recently reopened.

August 21, 1908. The new road being built between Hartsville and Macon County was progressing rapidly. The road was expected to run through Lafayette and on to Red Boiling Springs. Several construction groups, each acting under separate contracts, were building the road. Each contractor group was building about one mile of road.

The belief was that the road could be one of the best investments the two counties had ever made. It would tie Macon and Trousdale counties together and make travel between them easier, especially in the wintertime when up to then, the roads were mostly impassable.

July 30, 1909. Charles E. Bailiff of Nashville saw the lack of a railroad to Red Boiling Springs as an opportunity. He announced that he was establishing an "automobile line for the conveying" of passengers. He intended to start his service on August 1. Bailiff intended to make two or more "regular" daily runs between Gallatin and Dixon Springs, Tennessee (less than 25 miles), making connection with Louisville & Nashville trains at Gallatin. The travel time to Red Boiling Springs was expected to be "much improved." A person could leave Nashville by train in the morning, get off at Gallatin, take Bailiff's auto to Hartsville, and then go from Hartsville to Red Boiling Springs, and arrive at the resort in time for dinner.

By late August it was clear that the well-known entrepreneur from the Elmwood section of Nashville, Marvin Ford, was the driving force behind Bailiff's automobile line. Ford was also the chief financial backer of the enterprise. Called the Ford and Bailiff Rapid Transit Company, it had a capital investment of $10,000 (twice as great as the capital investment of the company proposing to build a railroad between Westmoreland and Red Boiling Springs).

The company already had a car in service, but it couldn't accommodate all that wanted to use it. To get more passengers to

Red Boiling Springs, Ford ordered "a mammoth 16-passenger car" at a staggering cost of $4,000 (almost $150,000 in today's currency). The giant machine would make daily trips between Carthage and Red Boiling Springs. The monster car could average about 15 miles per hour and could reach Red Boiling Springs in about 90 minutes. Compared to the four to six hours the trip took by hack make the car seem like "rapid transit" indeed. With the auto service, the trip from Nashville to Red Boiling Springs took less than 12 hours.

Marvin Ford was a true visionary. He said the time was coming when every community in the Upper Cumberland region would be connected by good roads. It is likely that many of those that heard him talk about the future thought he was crazy.

December 17, 1911. There was a proposed new highway from Glasgow, Kentucky to Scottsville, Kentucky and on to Red Boiling Springs. The surrounding counties were working on ways to connect to the new highway when it got to Red Boiling Springs.

July 19, 1913. A great of interest had developed concerning a "through pike" from Nashville by way of Gallatin, Hartsville, and Lafayette to Red Boiling Springs. Proponents of the road pointed out that "Red Boiling Springs is a fine summer resort, but many refuse to go and spend their summers at this place on account of the inconvenience of reaching it. They also pointed out that there were only 12 of the 72 miles between Nashville and Red Boiling Springs that needed improvement.

A meeting was planned at Red Boiling Springs for the purposes of "arousing greater interest" in the project and developing "some plan that may make the road possible." The Nashville Board of Trade promised to send "a large crowd of boosters to the meeting."

The belief was that there had to be something special done to create interest in the road. To create that interest, the Nashville Board of Trade planned a three-day automobile tour from Nashville to Red Boiling Springs. The five-vehicle caravan was scheduled to leave Nashville on Friday, August 1 and reach Red

Boiling Springs the next day. Then, the parade of cars would leave for home on August 3. The trip came in response to a letter the Board of Trade received from the editor of the *Macon County News*, Bedford C. Hix. The Nashville Automobile Club agreed to provide the cars. The itinerary called for the caravan to stop at Lafayette before embarking on the last leg of the trip.

On June 26, the Board of Trade received a telegram from W. G. Schamberger pledging that four other cars would join the caravan in Gallatin.

On July 29, the Board of Trade received a large poster with the following message:

"Road meeting at Red Boiling Springs, Saturday August 2 to make plans for building a good road from Lafayette to Red Boiling Springs, thus completing a fine highway from Nashville to Macon's famous springs. Big speaking by Nashville men and other good speakers. Biggest lot of automobiles ever in the upper country and the greatest good roads meeting we have ever known. Come on! Spend a day boosting Tennessee's most popular summer resort."

The caravan leaving Nashville included:

Car number 1: M. D. Stone of Jackson Motor Car Company and Charles J. Marthey.

Car number 2: M. H. Simmons and Albert Harnish.

Car number 3: W. L. Looney, representing the Nashville Businessmen's Association; O. H. Looney; B. Duke Gizzard, representing the Nashville Boosters Club; and S. M. Deal.

Car number 4: W. K. Boardman, representing the Cumberland Telephone and Telegraph Company; W. H. Peyton; C. C. Gilbert; and A. H. Cox.

Car number 5: (The Board of Trade Car), John Good, Vice President; E. S. Shannon, Secretary; Professor J. H. Draughton; Henry B. Morrow, Jr., representing Nashville newspapers.

The plan was for the colorfully decorated cars with streamers declaring "Nashville Offers Opportunity" to depart Goodlettsville, early in the morning of August 1, and go to Gallatin, then on to Hartsville, and to Lafayette. At Lafayette they would stop and lunch at Woodmore Hotel.

Although the weather was rainy, the roads were believed to be good enough to make the trip and the caravan left on time. The trip was "very enjoyable with exception of an accident which occurred a few miles from [Lafayette] when the tire of the machine occupied by M. H. Simmons and Albert Harnish" blew out and the car overturned. Both men were trapped under the car briefly before being rescued. Simmons, the car owner, wasn't seriously injured and the car received only minor damage.

Harnish, on the other hand, did suffer a broken rib and internal injuries. He received medical treatment and was then taken to the Woodmore Hotel. He was able to go on to Red Boiling Springs the following day and said he was "feeling fine" and not in any pain.

When the caravan reached Lafayette, there was an open-air rally on the town square. There were several well-received speeches followed by Hubert Carter offering a resolution endorsing the road project and another urging that the Gallatin interurban railroad be extended to Red Boiling Springs by way of Lafayette. There were no objections.

A severe storm during the afternoon made the road to Red Boiling Springs virtually impassable and only the racing car with Stone and Gizzard made it to Red Boiling Springs that evening. The others postponed their trip to the resort until the next morning. They spent the night at the Woodmore.

The caravan got underway early the next morning for the rally there where 5,000 people were expected to approve the road project. All the cars except one made it to Red Boiling Springs. The heavy seven-passenger touring car driven by Broadman "was not able to plow through the deep mud which covered the rough road. The motorists abandoned the car and went the remainder of the way in a surrey.

Some of those invited to speak at the Red Boiling Springs Good Roads Rally included: Elmer White of Hartsville; J. S. , W. A. Smith, J. L. Holland, J. D. L. Blankenship, and M. H. Allen, of Lafayette; John Gore, W. W. Draper, and D. M. Johnson of Gainesboro; Pat Burnley of Willard; H. H. Mayberry of Nashville;

and J. R. Smith, Charles Bancroft McClellan, and S. A. Chitwood of Red Boiling Springs.

H. H. Howser presided over the event that took place "in a beautifully shaded grove" at Cloyd Place. As one would expect, there was "plenty of water" for the thirsty at the meeting. From the outset, the expectation was that those at the meeting would pledge enough to pay for finishing the 12 miles of unimproved roads. The turnout of 1,000 was much lower than expected, but it still amounted to more than the population of Red Boiling Springs.

At the meeting, several citizens of Macon County formed the Nashville-Red Boiling Springs Highway Association. The officers of the organization were President, Charles Bancroft McClellan, Red Boiling Springs; Vice Presidents, Dr. M. H. Allen, Red Boiling Springs; Ed Myers, Carthage; E. L. White, Hartsville; and J. H. Carter, Pleasant Shade; Secretary: R. B. Draper, Red Boiling Springs; Publicity Secretary, Bedford C. Hix.

The citizens of Macon County pledged $6,000 toward the road project and the Macon County Court (legislative body) was expected to appropriate $6,000 more. One of those making a pledge was Gid Lowe of Nashville. Lowe took a subscription of $50 worth of stock, and he hoped to make a profit on his investment. Lowe stated that the road would have tollgates and would generate a "good dividend."

Other project proponents were less committal than Lowe. They said they believed the project would take "definite form" shortly and that construction would begin soon.

The guests from Nashville and elsewhere spent the night at the Donoho Hotel before returning home the next day. That is all but Simmons and Harnish. Simmons, who wasn't noticeably injured in the car crash spent a few days at the Donoho. Harnish, however, took two weeks at the resort to recuperate.

July 29, 1913. Not every pleasure trip to Red Boiling Springs ended happily. About 3 p.m., D. M. Grim of Nashville was driving through Lafayette on his way to Red Boiling Springs for a vacation. Along with Grim, his spouse, son, and future Tennessee

Supreme Court Justice Albert Bramlett Neil and Neil's spouse were in the car. The car frightened a horse belonging to Curley Snider and the animal wound up with both its front legs broken. The poor animal had to be put down.

Snider alleged that the car struck the horse and Macon County Sheriff Johnnie Hanes arrested Grim and charged him with cruelty to animals. The well-to-do Grim wanted the matter to end quickly. He gave Snider $175, and the charges were dropped immediately. The Grim party did not continue to Red Boiling Springs. Shaken, they returned to Nashville instead.

January 8, 1914. Construction of the through road from Nashville to Red Boiling Springs was yet to begin, but the "prospects were brighter than ever before." Those pushing the project had been working for six months to secure the necessary rights of way so the 12-mile stretch of road between Lafayette and Red Boiling Springs could be improved. The most positive recent news was that the Macon County Court had granted a franchise for the entire road. The Court also recommended that the road commissioners involved provide $1,000 toward building a large bridge on the route.

January 20, 1914. More people in Red Boiling Springs were getting cars. Two new automobile licenses were issued there. License number 14224 was issued to the Ford owned by the McClellan Brothers, and J. W. Patterson obtained license number 14225 for his Ford.

April 11, 1914. B. O. Hagan of Red Boiling Springs received license number 15295 for his Ford.

May 29, 1914. Getting from Nashville to Red Boiling Springs was not exactly easy, but it was easier than it had been in past years. The Ryman Steamer Line offered pleasure seekers options to get away from the city for a nice vacation at Red Boiling Springs. The ship *Henry Harley* departed Nashville every Tuesday and Friday at 5 p.m. and connected with the Allen

Automobile Line at Hartsville, Dickson Springs, and Carthage. After a cruise up the Cumberland River, vacationers boarded a car and continued to Red Boiling Springs. The Ryman Line charged nothing for handheld baggage or trunks, but there was a "reasonable" charge to transport trunks by car.

The Ryman Line (a Division of the Nashville Packet Company) also offered "a most delightful" round trip service aboard the *Jo Horton Fall*. The ship left Nashville every Monday and Thursday at 5 p.m. It docked at West Point in Smith County where passengers could take autos to Red Boiling Springs. The boat trip cost $3.50 and included berths and meals. The price of the car trip was an additional $3.50.

The General Manager of the Ryman Steamer Line was Paul Milton Ryman. Ryman's father, Captain Green Ryman built Nashville's famous Ryman Auditorium. Paul Ryman's office was at 104 Broadway in Nashville.

June 30, 1914. Interest in improving the 12-mile patch of road was still strong and it appeared certain to happen. In fact, the road was scheduled to be opened in early July, if "agreeable contracts" could be concluded.

July 11, 1914. The Louisville & Nashville Railroad offered one-way or round-trip tickets from Nashville to Red Boiling Springs. Pleasure seekers could board a train in Nashville at 8:05 a.m., get off in Hartsville, and then be driven to Red Boiling Springs by car, arriving at the resort at 1:30 p.m. The trip of less than six hours was the quickest possible way to get from Nashville to Red Boiling Springs.

Tickets were available at the City Ticket Office on Fourth Avenue North or at the Union Depot.

August 23, 1914. There was an announcement of an agreement between the Nashville-Gallatin interurban railroad and an automobile line to transport parties of any size from Gallatin to Red Boiling Springs "over good roads quickly."

August 30, 1914. Thomas H. White was the Secretary of the H. C. Pague Company in Nashville. The company distributed Lee tires throughout the area. In a publicity stunt, White drove his Ford from Nashville to Red Boiling Springs and back as quickly as he could. Even though he described the rural roads as "deplorable," White made the round trip in excellent time. Beginning the trip at 8 a.m. and ending it at 8 p.m., White transversed the trek of 72 miles each way in a mere 12 hours. His blazing average speed of 12 per hour astonished some regular drivers.

September 12, 1914. Red Boiling Springs residents receiving new automobile licenses were F. C. Allen & Son, license number 18622 for a Ford, and William Moss, number 18623 for his Ford. Both vehicles were to be used for commercial purposes.

September 15, 1914. James Moss of Red Boiling Springs wanted a Ford Runabout. He couldn't pay cash for one, but he thought he could make a fair trade. Moss manufactured wooden handles for axes, picks, and sledge handles. Moss offered to trade 15,000 unfinished handles for a second-hand Ford Runabout. He was even willing to add a little money to sweeten the deal if the handles didn't match the value of the car. Moss said the handles were already at a shipping point and their value would increase dramatically soon.

A new Ford Runabout in 1914 went for $400 and it is likely that Moss wanted to deal for a used one for about half the new price. That being the case, he was offering his unfinished handles for less than 2¢ each.

May 21, 1915. The Nashville Packet Company was encouraging Nashvillians to take excursions to Red Boiling Springs, first by the ship *Jo Horton Fall* up the Cumberland River and then on to the resort by automobile. The ship left Nashville on Tuesdays and Fridays at 5 p.m., and Saturdays at 4 p.m. It offered "delightful" scenery and onboard music. After the car trip, passengers arrived in Red Boiling Springs at 11 a.m. The round-trip cost was $6.75.

June 7, 1915. The Louisville & Nashville Railroad offered a round trip between Nashville and Red Boiling Springs, via train to Hartsville and by car from Hartsville to Red Boiling Springs. The train would leave Nashville at 8:05 a.m., arrive at Hartsville at 10 a.m., then the car to Red Boiling Springs would leave immediately and get to the resort at 1 p.m. The round-trip cost was $7.25.

June 24, 1915. More cars were coming to the Upper Country all the time. In Red Boiling Springs, Irvin Donoho received license number 23254 for his Ford.

July 15, 1915. The Tennessee Central Railroad offered round-trip tickets to Red Boiling Springs for $7.15. A 10¢ savings over the Louisville & Nashville rate.

May 4, 1916. One could still take a "delightful Upper Cumberland River Trip" aboard the *Jo Horton Fall* from Nashville to any one of several places on the river, and then by hired car on to Red Boiling Springs. The boat departed Nashville at 5 p.m. every Tuesday and Friday. The one-way price was $3.50 and $6.75 for the 320-mile round-trip to West Point in Smith County. Meals and berths were provided aboard the vessel.

One could also take the steamer *Henry Harley* via the same route taken by the *Jo Horton Fall* and at the same price. The *Henry Harley* offered dinner and breakfast during the overnight trip. It departed the wharf at "the foot of Broadway" every Monday and Thursday at 5 p.m.

July 8, 1918. Driving passengers from various railroad depots to Red Boiling Springs was a lucrative business and the competition between drivers was intense. The competition between drivers Robert Morgan Sr. and Archie Wilkes led to a deadly violent confrontation.

The two men were at the railroad terminal at Hartsville at about 9 a.m. on July 8 when they became embroiled in a dispute over which would transport a group of awaiting passengers to Red

Boiling Springs. Enraged, Morgan drew a gun and shot Wilkes. The severely wounded Wilkes was rushed to a Nashville hospital, but the doctors could not save him and he died on July 11. Wilkes was only 27.

May 15, 1919. The Louisville & Nashville Railroad was offering tickets to Red Boiling Springs for $7.68, plus the additional war tax. Evidently, the price included a $5 fee to take a car from the train station at Hartsville to the resort.

March 3, 1920. The Macon County Court (legislative body) empowered County Chairman, W. C. Gregory, to sign a contract with the Tennessee Highway Commission that provided for building the first federal/state highway across Macon County. The highway would run from near Westmoreland, through Lafayette, to Red Boiling Springs and on east to the Clay County line.

June 6, 1921. The Louisville & Nashville Railroad's summer rate from Nashville to Red Boiling Springs, including the War tax, was $8.07. One could purchase tickets at Nashville's Consolidated Ticket Office or at the Independent Life Building.

April 9, 1922. The Highway Committee of the Nashville Auto Club was a powerful lobbying group. The committee pushed the Tennessee State Highway Department to earmark funds to Macon County for improving the road between Lafayette and Red Boiling Springs. The Highway Committee pointed out that the road connected with some "important trade centers." Beyond that, the road was popular because of the number of motorists driving from Nashville to Red Boiling Springs during the vacation season.

May 21, 1922. The travel time from Nashville to Red Boiling Springs was about five hours. The Tennessee Central Railway offered "Double daily train service" to Red Boiling Springs for $6.85 round-trip passage including car service to the resort from

Carthage. Trains left Nashville at 9 a.m. and 4:30 p.m. daily. Travelers arrived at Red Boiling Springs at 2:10 p.m. and 9:30 p. m. Return trips to Nashville left the resort at 5:30 a.m. and 2 p.m. and arrived at Nashville at 10:55 a.m. and 7:45 p.m.

June 22, 1922. Not to be outdone, the Louisville & Nashville Railroad offered round-trip service from Nashville to Red Boiling Springs for $6.85. Passengers took cars from the train depot at Hartsville for the final leg of the trip to Red Boiling Springs.

June 25, 1922. Nashville Auto Club Secretary, C. H. Peay, related a recent trip he took to Red Boiling Springs. He reported that the roads were better than he expected them to be. He went from Nashville to Gallatin via the Jackson Highway, and then through Castalian Springs, Hartsville, Lafayette, and on to Red Boiling Springs. He returned over the same as far as Gallatin, where he took Long Hollow Pike to Goodlettsville and then on to Nashville.

Peay advised motorists to take Dixie Highway from Nashville to Goodlettsville and then turn right onto Long Hollow Pike and proceed on to Gallatin. Peay said there was a "good, oiled road to the Davidson County line" and a "good gravel road" on to Gallatin. From Gallatin to Hartsville, there was a "fair macadam road" that remained "passable in all weather." Macadam is similar to asphalt.

There was a "good gravel road" between Hartsville and Lafayette, and the gravel road from Lafayette to Red Boiling Springs was "fair." The biggest problem with the road from Lafayette to Red Boiling Springs was the fact that streams ran across it in several places. Water covered the road when it rained, but receded quickly. He said that one could average 20 miles per hour on the trip from Nashville to Red Boiling Springs (about three and a half hours total) and he encouraged motorists to make the trip.

June 25, 1922. Councils of the Good Roads Association were formed at Red Boiling Springs, Lafayette, and Hartsville. The Councils worked together to improve roads in the area.

June 25, 1922. Representatives of the Nashville Auto Club accompanied the Tennessee Highway Department Inspection Car across the road between Lafayette and Red Boiling Springs. Club members pointed out problems with the road along the way, and Highway Department officials promised to make needed improvements immediately. It was considered vital for the road to remain in good repair because of the traffic between Nashville and the resort.

August 20, 1922. The lobbying of the Nashville Auto Club was paying off in Macon County. The Tennessee Highway Department was busily repairing the road between Lafayette and Red Boiling Springs.

February 4, 1923. The N. E. West garage was the distributor for the Durant Motors Company in Red Boiling Springs. Durant Motors Company's primary automobile was called the Star Car. Between 1922 and 1928, Durant billed the Star Car as a reasonable alternative to the Ford Model-T. However, it could never match Ford's price. In 1923, the Star Car went for $443 while the Model-T sold for only $364. Then, in 1924, Ford cut its price to $265.

June 9, 1923. The Louisville & Nashville Railroad still offered roundtrips between Nashville and Red Boiling Springs for $6.85, but only until October 31. Passengers could leave the train at either Gallatin or Hartsville and continue to Red Boiling Springs by hired car. One-way trips were $3.74. Travelers left Nashville aboard Louisville & Nashville trains at 7:25 and 11 a.m. and arrived at Red Boiling Springs at 12:30 and 4 p.m.

June 23, 1923. The Tennessee Central Railway also offered roundtrips from Nashville to Red Boiling Springs. The Tennessee

Central carried passengers to Carthage and then transported them by car to Red Boiling Springs. The Tennessee Central made two runs each way daily. It left Nashville at 9 a.m. and 4:20 p.m. and arrived at Red Boiling Springs at 2:30 p.m. and 9:30 p.m. respectively. Travelers returning to Nashville left Red Boiling Springs at 5:30 a.m. and 2 p.m. and arrived back home at 10:55 a.m. and 7:45 p.m., respectively.

The downside of using the Tennessee Central was that it cost $7.15, which was 30¢ more than the Louisville & Nashville charged. The extra 30¢ was apparently hurting business and the Tennessee Central lowered rates to $6.85 in early July.

November 11, 1923. International Harvester sold heavy-duty trucks for farm use. In Red Boiling Springs, the Knight Brothers sold International Harvester trucks, including the Model 61. The Model 61 was a 3-ton vehicle that went for $3,400.

February 21, 1924. Although the roads around Red Boiling Springs were better than they had been in earlier times, they were far from good during inclement weather. Dick Martin, a travelling salesman representing Nashville's Hooper Grocery Company found that out the hard way. His car became hopelessly stuck in the muddy road a few miles from Red Boiling Springs. Unable to get his "Tin Lizzie" to move, he had to hire a farmer with a team of mules to pull the car to a local garage. Most salesmen operating in the Red Boiling Springs area delayed trips there when it was raining or snowing.

March 7, 1924. The McClellan Brothers sold a Ford truck to W. T. Howard. Howard already ran one truck to Nashville hauling freight for Macon County merchants including J. S. Bohanan and Son of the Galen community, and the McClellan Brothers. Macon County merchants required so much merchandise brought from Nashville that Howard needed a second truck to handle all the orders.

June 15, 1924. The Louisville & Nashville Railroad continued to offer round-trip service to Red Boiling Springs for $6.85, and one-way service for $3.74.

July 9, 1925. The car service working with the Louisville & Nashville transporting passengers from Hartsville to Red Boiling Springs was called the Red Boiling Springs Auto Company.

July 20, 1924. Tennessee Central Railroad did not hike its prices in 1924 either. Rates remained at $6.85. However, departure and arrival times had changed somewhat. In 1924, trains departed Nashville at 9 a.m. and 5:20 p.m. and arrived at Red Boiling Springs at 5:20 p.m. and 10:30 p.m. Cars left Red Boiling Springs at 4:30 a.m. and 2:00 p.m. and the trains from Carthage arrived at Nashville at 9:45 a.m. and 7:30 p.m.

November 9, 1924. State Highway 52 was still a gravel road in 1924. There had been a concerted effort to keep it open in Macon County and it was in good shape between Lafayette and Red Boiling Springs. However, in other areas, Highway 52 was not was not close to good. Between Celina and Livingston it was a "rough dirt road and not suitable for automobile traffic."

February 17, 1925. Reports were that work on the road between Red Boiling Springs to the Kentucky border would begin in the early spring. After it was finished, work would begin to extend the road to Tompkinsville, Kentucky. When that road was finished, there would be for the first time a "hard" road from Red Boiling Springs to Glasgow, Kentucky.

May 15, 1925. The Nashville Chamber of Commerce took over the functions of the Nashville Safety Council and threw itself into improving highway transportation in Middle Tennessee.

The Chamber heard from a committee from a group on the topic of "improvement of the roads between Nashville and Red Boiling Springs." The committee stated the resort was an "asset to Nashville and the entire state" and that a more passable road would open new territories for Nashville merchants. According to the committee, the improvement project would cost about $1 million (about $17.8 million in current dollars).

The Chamber of Commerce agreed to send its own committee to Red Boiling Springs to investigate to situation and report back with its findings.

On June 12, the committee returned to Nashville and reported its findings. Members praised State Highway Commissioner James G. Creveling Jr. for his efforts to improve travel between Nashville and Red Boiling Springs. They continued that state employees were making it one of the best roadways in Tennessee. They closed by encouraging state officials to continue their excellent work to improve roads.

June 13, 1925. A sign of improving road conditions was found in the fact that more vacationers were driving their personal vehicles to Red Boiling Springs. J. E. Jordan, along with his wife and children, made the trip of about 300 miles from their home in Sylacauga, Alabama to Red Boiling Springs in their family car.

June 16, 1925. Perhaps because of the competition from automobiles, the Louisville & Nashville Railroad was offering round-trip weekend fares from Nashville to Red Boiling Springs for only $4.50. Trains departed on Fridays and Saturdays and passengers were required to return on the following Monday. District Passenger Agent for the railroad, R. C. Wallis encouraged Nashvillians to "spend your weekend vacation at this splendid resort."

July 1, 1925. Several citizens of Red Boiling Springs and Carthage met with the Nashville Chamber of Commerce. They asked for the Chamber's aid in their efforts to build a new road between the two towns. Red Boiling Springs educator, Professor Thomas Perry, addressed the Chamber. Charles McClellan also attended the meeting.

July 4, 1925. Not every motor trip to Red Boiling Springs ended happily. Sometimes they ended tragically. Charles A Watkins, age about 37, his spouse Elizabeth, age about 29, and their children, Martha, age about 5, and Charles Franklin, age about 2, drowned in the Coosa River. The family had left Fort McPherson, Georgia on their way to Nashville to visit Elizabeth's mother and then on to Red Boiling Springs. Charles was unfamiliar with surroundings and he drove the car off the road and it plunged into the river near Leesburg Landing, Georgia.

July 30, 1925. Thomas Perry was so dedicated to building a new road from Red Boiling Springs to the Kentucky border that he went among those living along the proposed route and solicited pledges of contributions to facilitate its construction. Perry soon claimed that he had raised enough money to construct the road.

July 31, 1925. There were two major problems with the route between Nashville and Red Boiling Springs. One was there were not very many road signs along the way. The lack of signs was especially aggravating at intersections. The lack of signs remained a problem until at least 1982. The other major problem was that some curves were so sharp that they were difficult to navigate even at slow speeds.

August 2, 1925. The Nashville Auto Club had received so many inquiries about the best route to Red Boiling Springs that it released directions to the resort. According to the Auto Club a driver's best bet was to take Highway 6 from Nashville, go 26 miles on the good macadam and rock asphalt road to Gallatin. From Gallatin take Highway 25 over 15.5 miles of fair to good gravel road and 6.5 miles of new bituminous and macadam road to Hartsville. From Hartsville travel along Highway 52 for 18 miles on the good gravel road to Lafayette. Finally, from Lafayette take the fair gravel road the remaining 12 miles to Red Boiling Springs. The total trip was 78 miles.

August 4, 1925. Train service wasn't exactly irrelevant yet, but more city dwellers were taking weekend jaunts to Red Boiling Springs by car. The Nashville Auto Club related that "One of the most popular weekend trips is to Red Boiling Springs, famed Macon County health resort and recreation center."

October 3, 1925. While the road from Lafayette to Red Boiling Springs was usually passable, the horrendous pass between Red Boiling Springs to the Kentucky border could barely be called a road at all. An editorial writer in Nashville stated, "This short link ought to be put in shape before winter, especially in view of the work that is being planned on the Kentucky side of the line." The editorial continued, "If we are going to have gravel roads in the thinly populated counties, then it is essential that we have maintenance crews assigned to them and constantly at work. If the needed attention is not given to maintenance then the money and labor that has been extended on dirt and gravel road building is lost."

December 11, 1925. Citizens of the Flippin community of Monroe County, Kentucky were pushing for a gravel road to be built from there to Glasgow, Kentucky. The distance of the proposed road would be 20 miles. Seven miles of the route were already being graveled. Building the throughfare would connect Glasgow to Red Boiling Springs via a hard service road for the first time.

December 28, 1925. Nearly 100 citizens from the Tennessee counties of Macon, Jackson, Putnam, DeKalb, and Warren visited with Governor Austin Peay and acting Highway Commissioner Neil Bass. The group presented a plan to build a highway from the Kentucky border across a portion of Tennessee not served by railroads and on to the Georgia state line. The proposed road would travel from the Kentucky border to Red Boiling Springs and then over Jennings Creek and on to Gainesboro. From Gainesboro the road would run to Smithville and then either via Cookeville or Double Springs to Dibrell and on to McMinnville.

From there it would continue through Chattanooga to the Georgia border.

Macon Countians at the meeting included Henry Counts, Thomas Perry, Charles Bancroft McClellan, Dr. Frank Clark, W. A. Knight, and Bug Shoulders.

February 27, 1926. Thomas Petty called a mass meeting in Red Boiling Springs regarding the goal of building a new road from there to the Kentucky state line. At the meeting, committees were formed to raise funds to be applied to building the road. Petty was happy to inform the crowd that those living along the proposed road had promised to work one day out of ten building it. This was a major commitment because most of those pledging their services were farmers who would have to neglect their crops while they were working the road.

Improvement was also to be made on the road between Gibbs Crossroads and Red Boiling Springs.

April 23, 1926. The Blue Grass Bus Line filed for incorporation with $25,000 in capital stock. The aim of the new company was to link several Tennessee and Kentucky towns together by use of five passenger buses. Each bus could carry 15 passengers. Tennessee towns served by the bus company included Nashville, Gallatin, Red Boiling Springs, Hartsville, Carthage, and others. Some of the Kentucky towns served were Franklin and Scottsville. Blue Grass was purchasing new equipment as well as assuming the bus line and equipment of M. A. Jernigan.

April 27, 1926. The United States Senate adopted legislation to build a bridge across the Gainesboro-Red Boiling Springs Road in Jackson County. Tennessee Senator Lawrence D. Tyson presented the bill.

May 31, 1926. The Louisville & Nashville Railroad was still offering round-trip summer fares between Nashville and Red Boiling Springs for $6.85. The majority of the price was taken up by the car service to the resort from Gallatin or Hartsville.

June 1, 1926. The Consolidated Bus Terminal opened at the corner of Fifth Avenue and Commerce Street in Nashville. Eight bus companies merged to form the new enterprise. The Consolidated Bus Line planned to send out "150 cars a day, carrying approximately 1,250 passengers." Consolidated planned to service "50 or more towns within a 90 mile radius of Nashville."

Naturally, Red Boiling Springs was one of the towns served by the bus line. Buses left Nashville for Red Boiling Springs each day at 8 a.m. and 2 p.m. Then, left Red Boiling Springs for Nashville at 7 a.m. and 2 p.m.

December 16, 1926. Work was well underway on the road from the Kentucky border to Red Boiling Springs and on to Carthage. The road from Kentucky would link with Highway 52 about a mile from Red Boiling Springs. Another roadway would be built from Monoville in Smith County to Carthage, thus completing the road north and south.

February 3, 1927. Some thirty-five representatives of motor transportation companies convened at Nashville's Union Truck Terminal. The purpose of the meeting was to form a lobbying group dedicated to obtain legislative protection for their fast growing industry.

At a second meeting on February 7, about 100 representatives attended and choose a permanent committee to recommend trucking legislation to the state government. The Knight Brothers of Red Boiling Springs had representatives at both meetings.

July 11, 1927. Faced with stiff competition from bus services taking passengers directly to Red Boiling Springs, and with more people driving themselves to the resort, the Louisville & Nashville Railroad endeavored to remain relevant by lowering its fares. Round trip tickets on the railroad could be purchased from the Gallatin and Red Boiling Springs Auto Club for $5.90. One way tickets were $3.26.

August 6, 1927. Bakertown Hill between Red Boiling Springs and Gainesboro had been reduced until there was only a 6% grade. Before the roadwork was done, motorcars could not go over the hill and drivers had to be diverted through Willette. With the hill cut down the road could be graded and the distance between the two towns was reduced by seven miles.

August 20, 1927. A truck transporting Ajax tires lost one off its bed somewhere between Nashville and Red Boiling Springs. The tire, which was on an Oldsmobile rim, was valuable enough that the Ajax Company offered a reward for its return.

November 21, 1927. County committees of the American Automobile Association from Clay, Macon, Overton, Putnam, Sumner, and Trousdale met with Governor Henry H. Horton and State Highway Commissioner C. N. Bass. They were joined by representatives from the Nashville Auto Club. The purpose of the meeting was to discuss road development in the Upper Cumberland.

The delegation contended that paving highways in the Upper Cumberland was vitally important to business concerns in Nashville. They pointed out that paved highways would make it much easier and less expensive to transport livestock, timber, tobacco, and other commodities from the Upper Counties to Nashville markets. State Highway 52 was of especial importance because it was the sole highway from Hartsville to Lafayette, on to Red Boiling Springs, and through the heart of Clay County. The delegates held that maintaining Highway 52 adequately would increase commerce between Nashville and the Upper Region by millions of dollars annually.

Henry Counts and B. W. Chitwood attended the meeting on the behalf of Red Boiling Springs.

April 4, 1928. The Board of Directors of the Tennessee Good Roads Association met at Nashville's Hermitage Hotel and discussed their policy objectives. Among other things, the group proposed that state government "place the Tennessee Highway

Department on such a basis that its administration will be non-political, businesslike, and continuous, and that its finances will be adequate, safeguarded, and properly derived."

The plan continued that commissioners should be appointed by the Governor and confirmed by the State Senate. Additionally, the association called for $10 million to be set aside for road construction. The association conceded that putting its plan into operation would require a hike in the gasoline tax and the selling of state bonds.

B. W. Chitwood of Red Boiling Springs was a board member and he attended the meeting.

April 9, 1928. The Railway and Public Utilities Commission (later called the Public Service Commission) had taken jurisdiction over all property and passenger bus carriers in the state. The Commission mandated that all such carriers be certified to continue their operations. Middle Tennessee carriers could apply for certification beginning on April 9.

The only such carrier in Red Boiling Springs was the Knight Brothers Transfer Company. The Knight Brothers applied for certificates to transport both passengers and property between Red Boiling Springs and Lafayette, Hartsville, Gallatin, and Nashville.

April 12, 1928. The Rusco Company touted its transmission linings as being the best for gaining smooth operation of Ford automobiles. The Knight Brothers in Red Boiling Springs sold and installed Rusco transmission linings.

April 18, 1928. There was a grand ceremony for the beginning of construction of the Austin Peay Highway. About 3,500 hundred were at the ceremony. Dignitaries from across the state and residents from communities that had worked for the new highway to be built attended. Charles B. McClellan of Red Boiling Springs was one of the speakers.

The new hard surface highway would begin in Celina and then pass through Red Boiling Springs, Lafayette, Westmoreland,

Portland, Orlinda, Springfield, Cedar Hill, Adams, Clarksville, Dover, McKenzie, and other towns before ending at Brownsville in West Tennessee.

May 6, 1928. Fears arouse that the new Austin Peay Highway would bypass Red Boiling Springs. Tennessee State Highway Commissioner Harry S. Berry tried to put those concerns to rest. He told a large audience, "I've heard that it has been rumored around that the highway would not touch Red Boiling Springs. That is absurd. A highway of this kind could not be built without taking in such a resort, with its worldwide reputation."

June 29, 1928. Flooding across Middle Tennessee made many roads impassable. The Nashville Auto Club informed motorists that the only way to get from Nashville to Cookeville was to go to Red Boiling Springs and from there drive through Gainesboro and on to Cookeville.

October 16, 1929. Evert Spears appeared before the Tennessee Railroad and Public Utilities Commission and protested unaccredited bus services. Spears owned a bus line that operated from Livingston via Celina, Moss, Red Boiling Springs, and on to Toledo, Ohio. He requested that the commission take action to prevent uncertified bus services from operating along the same or similar routes as his.

November 19, 1929. The Tennessee Railroad and Public Utilities Commission certified the Knight Brothers Safety Coach Line of Red oiling Springs. The certification allowed Knight Brothers to operate between Nashville and Carthage via Red Boiling Springs, Hartsville, and Monoville. The Union Transfer Company of Knoxville had opposed granting the certificate. It claimed it already provided adequate service to the area.

Losing its Upper Cumberland monopoly didn't harm the Union Transfer Company very much. Now known as the Union Transfer and Storage Company, it is still in business today.

November 13, 1930. Consolidated Bus Lines ran through several cities and towns between Nashville and Knoxville. It offered low rates and insured every passenger. Consolidated advertisements made a point of stating that it made connections to Red Boiling Springs daily.

June 7, 1930. Governor Henry Horton and other dignitaries were invited to attend a meeting of the Austin Peay Memorial Highway Association at Springfield, Tennessee. The Red Boiling Springs chapter sent a delegation.

September 11, 1931. The Tennessee Railroad and Public Utilities Commission heard a request from the B. & T. Bus Lines for a certificate to operate a service between Springfield and Red Boiling Springs via Orlinda, Portland, and Lafayette.

September 13, 1931. Traffic to and from Red Boiling Springs was increasing and with more automobiles on the roadways. Of course, the increased traffic meant more accidents as well. Sumner County Sheriff William M. "Kenno" Keen and his son Loyd were returning to Gallatin after a trip to Red Boiling Springs. The Sheriff lost control of his car in a sharp curve. The car crashed into a ditch and flipped over. Lloyd was stunned, but not seriously injured. The Sheriff's condition was worse. He was knocked unconscious and suffered other "painful injuries."

The Sheriff and his son were transported to the office of Dr. L. M. Woodson in Gallatin for treatment. Dr. Woodson was forced to amputate one of Sheriff Keen's mangled fingers.

Sheriff Keen left office in 1932 and he committed suicide in 1940.

May 30, 1932. The Fourth District Rural Mail Carriers Association held their annual convention at Red Boiling Springs. Three members of Congress, Democrats Joseph W. "Jo" Byrns and John Ridley Mitchell, and Republican James W. "J. Will" Taylor were scheduled to address the meeting, but Byrnes and Taylor cancelled their visits.

Some 350 people attended the convention and the Red Boiling Springs brass band furnished music.

July 13, 1932. Alice Capshaw, age 76, died at Cookeville. On July 10, after a stay at Red Boiling Springs, she, her driver, and two other guests of the resort were going along the road near Hermitage Springs when the automobile they were in went over an embankment and crashed. Capshaw was the only person hurt in the accident, but her injuries were severe. She was admitted to a hospital and soon developed pneumonia which led to her death.

Alice Capshaw was the daughter of the first Trustee of Putnam County, Tennessee. Her three sons were all attorneys. One of them was also a minor politician in New York City.

July 18, 1932. Getting from Nashville to Red Boiling Springs had never been easier. For those with cars, "excellent" highways led there and one could motor to the resort in about two hours. For those that didn't want to drive, bus connections were readily available at modest rates.

July 24, 1932. The management of Consolidated Bus Lines whose motto was "Go by Bus, Cheaper, Quicker, Safer," encouraged vacationers to "Ride the bus to Red Boiling Springs and spend an enjoyable weekend." The bus line sweetened the deal by offering special round-trip rates of $3.50 for those taking the "Red Boiling Springs Special." The ticket wasn't just good for a weekend. The return tickets would be honored until September 15.

Buses left Nashville for Red Boiling Springs daily at 8 a.m. and 3:30 p.m. Buses left Red Boiling Springs for Nashville at 7 a.m. and 2:30 p.m.

January 28, 1933. Consolidated Bus Lines was offering a special round-trip rate to Red Boiling Springs. The $2.25 round-trip fare was only 25¢ more than a one-way ticket. In June, the bus line returned to its summer rate of $3 for a round-trip ticket.

Consolidated management continued to contend that taking a bus to Red Boiling Springs was cheaper and safer than driving there.

June 7, 1934. A Nashville court awarded Malcom Massey of Red Boiling Springs $5,000 for injuries he received in an accident that occurred in 1928. Massey was struck and injured by a bus that he was about to board at Mansker's Creek in Davidson County. A truck owned by the firm of Gregory and Oldham plowed into the back of the stopped bus knocking it into Massey. Massey suffered a fractured skull and an injury to one eye. The court held Gregory and Oldham liable.

December 10, 1934. The summer season was long since ended, but the Consolidated Bus Lines was still pushing its low round-trip rates to Red Boiling Springs.

May 30, 1935. The Tennessee Railroad and Public Utilities Commission denied the Southern Greyhound bus line the ability to open a new route between Nashville and Louisville. The ruling stood to impact Red Boiling Springs negatively. Had the route been granted passengers from Ohio and Kentucky could have gone directly to the resort by bus.

June 25, 1939. Consolidated Bus Lines continued to claim that its service was less expensive than driving was. To prove it, the bus service lowered its rates between Nashville and Red Boiling Springs. One-way fares were $1.25 and round-trip tickets were $2.25.

May 14, 1940. After fielding several complaints, the Tennessee Railroad and Public Utilities Commission hit the Consolidated Bus Lines with a "show cause" order requiring the company to prove why its schedules, equipment, and services should not be improved between Nashville and Red Boiling Springs via Gallatin. If Consolidated wouldn't make the improvements and couldn't show why it shouldn't be required to, the commission could withdraw the company's certification and force it to discontinue service.

May 4, 1941. Consolidated Bus Lines had taken passengers to Red Boiling Springs for 21 years, and despite changes in the transportation business, and other problems, it continued to do respectable business. Company President J. E. Evins was proud that his buses had carried "more than three times the population of Tennessee without a single passenger fatality."

The bus line specialized in chartered trips "short or long" and promised passengers comfortable and roomy seats, bonded drivers, and courteous service.

Consolidated used "pusher" type buses which had engines in the rear and were bigger than other buses.

August 14, 1942. A person in Nashville was looking for a driver to take him to Red Boiling Springs on either Aug 14th or the 15th. The driver would not receive any compensation and would have to provide references.

September 30, 1944. There was a big campaign kickoff rally at Cookeville for United States Representative Jim McCord. McCord was the Democratic nominee for Governor. The event wasn't free but hundreds were expected to purchase tickets and attend. Getting to the event could be a problem because several major roads between Nashville and Cookeville were closed for repairs. Those living north of Nashville were advised to go to Cookeville via Red Boiling Springs.

McCord won the election with ease.

4. A Railroad to Red Boiling Springs

There were numerous efforts to bring a railroad line through Red Boiling Springs. Proponents of a railroad contended that it would be good for business, especially the lumber industry, and would be a boon to the hotel industry as well. This chapter takes a brief look at the decades long efforts to get a railroad through Red Boiling Springs.

February 25, 1903. The idea of a rail line to Red Boiling Springs had been debated and rejected several times in the past [See *The Fountain of Youth at Red Boiling Springs, Tennessee: Part 1*], but it was under consideration again. The Nashville, Chattanooga & St. Louis Railroad sent a team of engineers from Lebanon to Rome, Smith County, Tennessee at the junction s of Round Lick Creek and the Cumberland River. The goal was to run a rail line from Smith County to Red Boiling Springs, and then to the Kentucky coal and timber fields. The belief was that the railroad would begin putting down tracks in a short time. As in the past, most thought a railroad line through Red Boiling Springs would help the resort and spa business continue to thrive.

March 9, 1903. Getting a railroad remained a complicated proposition. Running a rail line from Smith County Tennessee to Red Boiling Springs was an attractive idea, but there was a major problem. There was a need for a new bridge across the Cumberland River strong enough to carry trains from Carthage. While the Tennessee Central Railroad promised that if the bridge was built, it would run tracks across it, the taxpayers of Smith County would have to pay for the bridge's construction. The cost of building such a bridge was put at $60,000 (more than $2.1 million in today's currency). Proponents of the bridge were confident that the Smith County Court (legislative body) would appropriate the funds during its April session.

August 5, 1904. "Reliable sources" were certain that the Tennessee Central Railroad would soon extend a rail line from Carthage, Tennessee, through Gordonsville, to Red Boiling Springs, and on to the coal fields and timber lands of Kentucky.

The bridge across the Cumberland River near Carthage [See above] would still have to be built, but the well-informed people in Smith County felt it was "likely" that the bridge would be erected.

Hotel owners in Red Boiling Sprigs wanted the railroad to pass through because it would add to their profits. Smith County leaders wanted the new line too. These leaders promised that "Every effort will be put forth by the citizens of this county to encourage the contemplated step."

This effort to get a rail line to Red Boiling Springs failed as well.

April 18, 1905. Observers felt that the one thing Macon County lacked was for an "electric train railroad company to build the road to Gallatin and on to Lafayette and the famous Red Boiling Springs." Then, according to the observers, Macon County would be in Tennessee's "front rank."

May 22, 1905. An editor in Nashville pointed to what they felt were the reasons a railroad should run through Red Boiling Springs: "One of the largest and most valuable sections of country for a railroad which has none lies north of Cumberland River between the Louisville & Nashville and the Cincinnati Railroads. It is a heavily timbered section and is filled with saw, stave and handle mills, turning out an immense amount of stuff that has to be stacked and kept until the boats can navigate the river or else be hauled by wagon on average about fifty miles. In short, there is more freight going in and coming out of this section with less transportation facilities than in any county in Tennessee or Kentucky."

The editor continued, "The famous Red Boiling Springs is located in this section and the passenger traffic to and from this hotel health resort, if there was a railroad touching it ... would be no small item." The editor felt the railroad should tie Red Boiling Springs to Nashville, Tennessee and Corbin, Kentucky via the Cincinnati Southern Railroad.

One of the routes most discussed and investigated "would come from Monticello, Kentucky, to Albany, Kentucky, cross the Cumberland River between Martinsburg, Kentucky and Celina, Tennessee, and on by Red Boiling Springs, Lafayette and Gallatin to Nashville."

The editor believed that "The people in this section are very much interested in this railroad and would do anything to secure it."

July 25, 1905. The news was that engineers had completed surveying a new rail line from Corbin, Kentucky on the Cincinnati Southern Railroad, to Westmoreland. From there it would connect with the Chesapeake & Nashville Railroad.

The proposed rail line would run through Red Boiling Springs, Lafayette, Monticello, Kentucky and Burnside, Kentucky. The line would give an outlet to the "upper counties" that had no railroad outlet. The railroad would be called The Kentucky & Cumberland River in Kentucky, and in Tennessee, the Tennessee & Northern.

"Good authority" had it that the bonds for the railroad had been "floated" and that the new line was an "assured fact." The source continued that work on the line from Westmoreland to Corbin would begin immediately and pushed as quickly as possible. The counties which the new line would run through were rich in coal, minerals, and timber and giving them an outlet which would of "untold value to them and to Nashville."

September 22, 1905. A dispatch from Red Boiling Springs stated that property there, including most of the choice land, had been recently purchased by the Louisville & Nashville Railroad.

The message continued that the company intended to build a rail line to Red Boiling Springs before the summer of 1906.

The dispatch could not be verified as authentic, but the consensus was that "the officers of the Louisville & Nashville have purchased the property with the understanding that the railroad company is to build a new line there. At present, the Tennessee Central is the nearest line to Red Boiling Springs, Carthage being twenty miles distant, being the nearest point."

The line, it was believed, would be a boon to Red Boiling Springs because "the water at the springs is said to contain fine medicinal qualities, and those who have visited the springs state it would attract many thousands of people if fitted up with proper accommodations. It is very likely that some handsome hotels and many other improvements will be made there if the Louisville & Nashville is behind the enterprise."

As it turned out, the dispatch was based on rumor, not fact.

September 28, 1905. The Sumner County, Tennessee the Register of Deeds in Gallatin transferred the title of the Chesapeake & Nashville Railroad from Walter A. Webber of New York City to William A. Northup of Louisville, Kentucky. The purchase included the entire 35-mile line from Gallatin to Scottsville, Kentucky, and the branch running from Rogana in Sumner County, Tennessee 11 miles to Hartsville in Trousdale County, Tennessee. The selling price was $600,000 ($300,000 each for the railroad and its equipment). In today's dollars, that was about $21.2 million.

The news of the sale of the Chesapeake & Nashville Railroad from Gallatin to Scottsville coupled with the previous news that the Louisville & Nashville Railroad had made a large property purchase in Red Boiling Springs caused a stir in Macon County. A group of citizens in Lafayette inquired of *The Nashville American* editor about the stories. The answer was that William A. Northup was connected to the legal department of the Louisville and Nashville Railroad. The editor also pointed out that the story of the purchase of the Chesapeake & Nashville originated with the *Louisville Courier-Journal*.

October 7, 1905. There had been no official confirmation from an official source that the Louisville & Nashville Railroad was the "real purchaser of the Chesapeake & Nashville Railroad," but most observers "confidently believed" that the reports were true. Another "good source" claimed that the Louisville & Nashville Railroad intended improve the property, extend the line north, connect it to the Glasgow, Kentucky line, and lay a double track between Gallatin and Louisville.

Proponents of the new line contended that it would reach counties, such as Macon in Tennessee that had no railroad connections, reach Red Boiling Springs and other resort towns, open new mines, and give the railroad a "splendid local line."

Again, even though railroad representatives had made no official pronouncement of its plans, it was believed "pretty certain" that the double line would be finished in 1907 or 1908.

March 22, 1906. Since no railroad had made it to Red Boiling Springs yet, a different group decided to form a new company and run a trolley line through the town. A charter was granted at Frankfort, Kentucky for the purpose of running an electric trolly line from Stanford, Kentucky to Gallatin, Tennessee. The trolley line would wind through the Kentucky towns of McKinney, Liberty, Burkesville, and Tompkinsville. It would then cross into Tennessee and pass through Red Boiling Springs, Lafayette, and Hartsville before reaching Gallatin. The incorporators stated that the line might extend into Nashville should the projected trolley service there not be built.

The capital stock of the new company was placed at $150,000 (more than $5.1 million in today's currency). The incorporators were listed as W. G. Schamberger of Gallatin, J. I. White, Dr. Peyton, Harvey Helms, Judge Bailey, and others from Stanford, Kentucky.

Construction of the trolley line, which was expected to haul both passengers and freight, was expected to begin within a month.

As with all the previous projected lines running through Red Boiling Springs, no trolley line ever came through.

August 27, 1906. There had been so many rumors of rail lines coming through Red Boiling Springs that few could keep track of them all, but every time a new rumor emerged hopes rose. The latest rumor seemed promising.

J. A. Bailey, "a representative of Chicago capitalists" visited Scottsville, Kentucky and the towns adjoining it. Bailey said he was attending to the interests of an unnamed electric railway company. He said the company was considering running a line from Bowling Green, Kentucky through Scottsville, to Lafayette, and on to Red Boiling Springs.

Bailey told skeptical citizens that those behind the project "mean business" and were certain to build the line. Bailey spoke to leaders in Scottsville and said the only requirements remaining were obtaining the necessary rights of way and payment for the survey of the route. He said he had travelled the prospective route and the people along the way were "enthusiastic" and obtaining the rights of way and paying for the survey would be "no trouble."

It was apparent that Bailey expected the communities involved to secure the rights of way and pay for the survey before the railway company did anything. As all the others had, this promise of a railroad coming to Red Boiling Springs soon evaporated.

June 20, 1907. There were conflicting and confusing reports coming from the Southern Railway Company. Rumors that the railroad company would lay a line from Lebanon, Tennessee to Red Boiling Springs and other parts of the "upper country" were fueled by the fact that the civil engineers working for the railroad had been headquartered in Lebanon for three or four weeks and they had surveyed much of the upper country.

Yet, the leaders of the Southern Railway Company were mostly closemouthed about their intentions. They refused to say exactly what they had planned other than straightening out some curves and reducing some of the steep grades along the line. When asked if they were considering putting down new tracks through the Tennessee towns of Lafayette, Red Boiling Springs, Alexandria, and Sparta, they were noncommittal.

The common belief was that if the Southern Railway wouldn't build the new line, that the Nashville, Chattanooga, & St. Louis Railroad Company would. The company had already surveyed a route from Sparta to Red Boiling Springs and most thought it wanted to build the line that would no doubt be profitable.

But the Louisville & Nashville Railroad Company presented a problem. The Louisville & Nashville controlled the rails between Nashville and Lebanon and the fear was that it would veto the project as it was believed to have done previously.

Whether the Louisville & Nashville Railroad nixed the project or not, once again no railroad line was built to Red Boiling Springs.

September 2, 1907. There was still another promise of a railroad line coming to Red Boiling Springs. The group planning to make tracks to Red Boiling Springs this time was called the Nashville & Northeastern Railroad. It was headquartered in Celina, Tennessee. The stockholders met in Celina and chose the following to be on the board of directors: Samuel Woodward, Cincinnati (President); James Denton Somerset, Kentucky (Secretary); S. B. Anderson, Celina (member); W. T. Moore, Celina (member).

The proposed line would run from Corbin, Kentucky to Clarksville, Tennessee with "intermediate points" at the Kentucky towns of Albany, Burnside, and Monticello, and at the Tennessee communities of Lillydale, Celina, Spivey, Red Boiling Springs, Lafayette, Westmoreland, Buck Lodge, and Springfield. The directors expressed hope that the initial survey would be completed by December.

Once again those who got their hopes up saw them crash back to earth when no choo-choo rumbled into Red Boiling Springs.

May 10, 1909. The "railroad through Red Boiling Springs" talk flared up again. This time the "expert" observers believed that it just might happen. The news was that Macon County citizens had "raised enough money by private subscription" to nearly pay for a survey through the county. The belief was that the Cumberland

River Railroad Company would lay track beginning in the eastern part of Macon County near Red Boiling Springs, take it through Lafayette, and on to Westmoreland. Once at Westmoreland, the Cumberland River Railroad would link the new line with the Louisville & and Nashville Railroad and be able to go all the way to Nashville and beyond.

May 12, 1909. The story about the Cumberland River Railroad Company building a railroad line was incorrect, but there was a new railroad company being formed that had virtually the same goal in mind. A group of Macon County citizens applied for a corporate charter for an entity they called the Westmoreland & Red Boiling Springs Railroad. The incorporators were W. A. Smith (President), E. K. Lamb (Secretary), Albert R. Dean (Treasurer), H. C. Smith, and J. B. Kemp. A. J. Bright of the Bright Construction Company was the chief engineer for the project and J. L. Holland was the Corresponding Secretary. The capital stock in the company of $5,000 was surprisingly small.

The application for the charter was flawed and it wasn't granted right away. It was corrected and granted on May 20.

On August 23, A. J. Bright departed Nashville for Lafayette to take charge of the surveying party that was plotting the path for the proposed railroad.

On September 7, there was a huge crowd in Lafayette at a meeting about the railroad coming through Macon County. Chief engineer A. J. Bright gave an account of the survey between Westmoreland and Lafayette. Bright produced charts showing where the line would run, the "percentage of grades, depth of cuts, etc." Those in attendance were "very much encouraged" by Bright's report and most thought that this time the dream of a railroad would become a reality. Bright promised that a survey from Lafayette to Red Boiling Springs would begin "at once."

Bright said he expected the survey through Red Boiling Springs to be finished before October 1. He continued that he was finding a "much nicer route for the road" than he had expected and that "the new line can be built for a very little money compared with other lines in Tennessee." The citizens of Macon had already raised enough money to pay for the surveys through the purchase of subscriptions.

The residents of Monroe County, Kentucky were "jubilant" over the prospect of a railroad line running along the Tennessee/Kentucky border between Lafayette and Red Boiling Springs. It would bring them 15 miles closer to a railroad and would change their shipping point from Glasgow to Red Boiling Springs.

It appeared that a rail line through Red Boiling Springs was indeed going to happen. By September 24, Bright had finished the survey for the entire line between Westmoreland and Red Boiling Springs and had returned to Nashville for a few days. He expected to return to Macon County on September 27 to finish securing the necessary rights of way.

The proposed line would run 30 or so miles between Westmoreland and Red Boiling Springs and was expected to be a boon to the resort because pleasure seekers would find it much easier and much quicker to get there by rail than the long trip that required several changes of conveyance they had to endure then. Beyond that, after the initial line was finished, the leaders of the Westmoreland and Red Boiling Springs Railroad intended to extend it into Kentucky.

On October 8 Bright was still in Macon County working out the details of the new railroad. He expected his work to be finished in two weeks. Things didn't go as smoothly as Bright had hoped. On October 30, Bright was still trying to secure the necessary rights of way to build the rail line. The optimistic engineer stated that 75% of the rights of way would be "donated by the property owners." The amount of land Bright wanted donated was very valuable, but the engineer didn't seem to think it would be an issue.

The Corresponding Secretary of the Westmoreland and Red Boiling Springs Railroad, J. L. Holland, was busily promoting the company. On December 4, Holland gave an interview in which he discussed the new Railroad. The question and answer session went like this:

Question: Is the enterprise doing well?

Answer: Yes, we have a splendid enterprise, plenty of determination, favorable conditions, and we feel we are bound to be successful.

Question: Where will the line run?

Answer: Our road will extend from a connection with the L & N at Westmoreland via Lafayette to Red Boiling Springs, a distance of 30 miles. All this road (except two miles in Sumner County) will be in Macon County running lengthwise through the center of our county.

Question: Is the project progressing well?

Answer: The survey has already been made, accurate bearings have been taken, and our engineer and draftsmen are now working on the map and projected profile.

Question: Will the line run well?

Answer: Yes, our profile is splendid, much better, even than we anticipated. You see, the entire line is on top of the level ridge, which separates the Cumberland and Barren rivers. The maximum grade is one and one-half percent, and grades of this kind are very short, and may be cut down, but are so arranged that they are easily overcome by the momentum from each other.

Question: Will the railroad include bridges and tunnels?

Answer: No, no, we have no tunnels, no bridges.

Question: Will the railroad be expensive to build?

Answer: The ties are all standing in the woods near the road, and construction will be cheap.

Question: Will the railroad make a profit?

Answer: Will it pay? Now, you have struck the most interesting part of the matter. We have a county as good as most of the counties of the state. Here at Lafayette is a town of more than a thousand people, which is at present the largest county seat in the state, having neither railroad nor river facilities. Red Boiling Springs is known by everybody to be unexcelled as a health resort by any springs in the United States (naturally so, I mean). I have frequently seen one hundred loads of lumber passing through this town on a single day. You understand we are here in the heart of a choice section of Tennessee's famous hardwood district, and the possibilities in the way of timber products of all kinds are practically unlimited. It is *our* timber that keeps the L & N going at Hartsville, and has made Hartsville one of the largest shipping points for lumber in the state. Besides this, we have splendid agricultural and horticultural resources. The other counties around us are without railroads, and this road would serve a population of more than 40,000, and of course it is bound to pay well.

On January 25, 1910, A. J. Bright was enroute back to Lafayette to "present the plans, specifications, etc." to the parties contemplating building the railroad through Macon County. Bright said he "had figured out the cost of building the road, even to the yardage and spurs." However, he didn't reveal what the cost would be. Bright continued that if his report was accepted, work on the railroad would begin that spring or as soon as the weather permitted.

Spring came right on time; but the railroad never did.

April 16, 1912. Rumors of a railroad, this time an interurban (electric) railway, or trolly line, was back in the news. The story was that a new electric rail was planned, but that the exact route was uncertain. One plan called for the line to connect Gallatin, Hartsville, Dixon Springs, Lafayette, and Red Boiling Springs. Another plan had the line running from Gallatin to Westmoreland and then eastward through Epperson Springs, Lafayette, and on to Red Boiling Springs. There was also a plan to run the line by way of Westmoreland and Scottsville, Kentucky, or by the Tennessee communities of Fountainhead and Portland to the terminal point in Gallatin.

The new corporation formed to build the line was called the Cumberland Valley & Interstate Railway Company. The incorporators were Harris Brown, Vice President of the First National Bank of Gallatin; S. M. Young, Smith County Court Judge; M. L. Wright, President of the Bank of Hartsville; William Hall, Cashier of the First National Bank of Gallatin; William Brown, Assistant Cashier of the First National Bank of Gallatin; W. G. Schamberger, President of the Sumner County Bank and Trust Company; Y. A. Allen, President of the People's National

Bank of Gallatin; Ed S. Payne of the Enon community, Macon County; and A. F. and Pat F. Burnley, owners of a tobacco factory in the Willard community, Trousdale County.

While Red Boiling Springs had been surveyed several times for a "steam railroad," it appeared that if any kind of line came through, it would be an interurban railroad.

The proponents of the line repeated the oft-stated reasons they thought a railroad would be good for the area.

July 18, 1912. The plans for the interurban line connecting Gallatin, Tennessee to Kentucky via Red Boiling Springs was still alive, but the construction was "contingent on the wishes and the interests of the people living along the route." Observers contended that the line "will probably be built if the people indicate that they really want" a railroad.

September 3, 1912. The *Macon County News* editorialized that the subscription fund for surveying a railroad route from Hartsville to Lafayette and then from Lafayette to Red Boiling Springs was "growing steadily, but not as rapidly as it should." The editorial continued, "There are a number of men over the county who are interested in a railroad and who are willing to make a survey but are just waiting for something to happen before they move." The editor then demanded, "If you want a railroad, you had better subscribe to this survey fund and help make something happen."

There was minimum donation to the fund requested, and those in charge of the subscription revenue promised to provide itemized statements detailing how the money was spent.

February 22, 1913. The interurban railway "from Nashville by way of Gallatin, Westmoreland, Epperson Springs, Lafayette, Red Boiling Springs, and on to Kentucky" was still being "seriously considered." The story was that those in charge of the effort were moving along with the "preliminary steps leading up to the actual construction" of the railway. They assured all interested parties that the road would be built. The line, if built, would, so they said, "in time, become a part of the contemplated system of transportation that will bring about a community of interest in [the] Cumberland valley which will more equalize opportunities in all sections affected."

August 1, 1913: At a town meeting in Lafayette, a group of citizens endorsed a resolution urging that the Gallatin interurban railroad be extended to Red Boiling Springs by way of Lafayette.

February 27, 1916. The quest of three decades to get a railroad line to Red Boiling Springs continued. A group applied for a charter to incorporate the Nashville, Hartsville & Red Boiling Railroad Company. The proposed line would run from Hartsville, through Lafayette and on to Red Boiling Springs. Under the terms of the charter, the trains, which would link with the Louisville & Nashville Railroad at Hartsville, could be either electric or steam powered, but the understanding was that the incorporators intended to operate an electric line.

The incorporators of the company were John C. Shofner, Howard Andrews, Perkins Baxter, J. C. Collins, W. M. Long, and J. M. Wilson. They announced that they would offer 5,000 shares of stock at $10 per share.

March 14, 1916. J. C. Collins of Nashville, the Secretary of the Nashville, Hartsville & Red Boiling Railroad Company spoke at a mass meeting on Public Square in Lafayette. Many prominent residents expressed support for building the railroad through Macon County. The belief was that if the company made a "fair and reasonable proposition" the Macon County Court would approve it.

March 29, 1916. There was another mass meeting on Lafayette's Public Square concerning the proposed railroad through Macon County. The meeting was organized by the Macon County Railroad Boosters and most of the crowd appeared enthusiastic about the prospects of a rail line. They were confident the if the Nashville, Hartsville & Red Boiling Railroad

Company presented a "fair proposition" that building the rail line was a certainly.

April 4, 1916. At the third mass meeting in Lafayette within a month, leaders of the Nashville, Hartsville & Red Boiling Railroad Company presented their proposal for the line. Word was that the crowd was "enthusiastic" about the plan. The spokesmen for the company promised to build the railroad from Hartsville to Lafayette and on to Red Boiling Springs if Macon County voters voted to approve $75,000 in bonds and purchased $50,000 in stock (the 5,000 shares at $10 each mentioned earlier). Again, it appeared that those at the meeting were mostly in favor of building the railroad. Additionally, several Macon County Court members stated their approval of a bond issue and they promised to put the matter before the voters "as soon as the opportunity avails."

Once again, no railroad ever came.

July 15, 1917. The dream of a railroad to Red Boiling Springs wasn't dead. The belief was that even though it was ready well-known as one of the top resorts in the United States, Red Boiling Springs would "become the most popular resort in the country" when it finally got a railroad. It never did.

5. Gold, Silver, and Oil, Oh My!

Finding gold or striking oil and making millions are the stuff of dreams. In the Red Boiling Springs are such dreams, though never fully realized, abounded. This chapter looks at some of the stories, mythical or not, of gold, silver, and oil reserves in and around Red Boiling Springs.

November 4, 1905. While the prospect of a rail line slicing through Red Boiling Springs in 1905 was the biggest news in the county, an old myth was still getting interest – Macon County's lost silver mine.

Stories of a large vein of silver in the area began with the Native American population before 1800. Legend has it that a Native American told a group of white men at Carthage, the county seat of the area at the time, that the silver mine was located at the head of Jennings Creek. He continued that if the white people could find it, they could mine enough silver to shoe all their horses with it. The story didn't cause a silver rush, but the story wasn't forgotten either.

Another story is that about 1800, a Spainard did find the silver strike. The tale is that one day a group of hunters from Smith County entered a large canebrake at the head of Jennings Creek and came upon a Spainard camped under an overhanging cliff. The Spainard invited the hunters to make camp with him and they agreed. The hunters shared camp with the Spainard for the next few days.

The hunters noticed that the Spainard carried a leather bag which he handled with care and never allowed out of his sight. The Spainard refused to talk about the bag, but whatever it contained was very heavy. Even though the leather bag was no bigger than a half bushel meal sack, the Spainard had to carry it on his shoulders and when he walked with it, he staggered under its weight. He could not carry the bag very far without having to stop and rest.

When they broke camp, the Spainard told the hunters that he was going to Mexico. He climbed into his little canoe, waved goodbye, and rowed down the stream, never to be seen again.

There was a boy in the hunting party named Neil McKinniss. The other hunters evidently forgot about the strange encounter with the Spainard, but McKinniss did not. After he was grown, he returned to the place and purchased it. He explored his property and at the point where the hunters met the Spainard under the overhanging cliff, McKinniss found a natural tunnel that extended through a hill to the other side. The tunnel was much larger on one end than on the other and because of its appearance, it came to be called the "Rock House." Despite his efforts, McKinniss didn't find any precious metals at or around the Rock House.

Then around 1840, a trader from the area was in New Orleans on business when he came across another Spainard. When the Spainard learned that the trader was from the area, he inquired about the Rock House. The Spainard was keenly interested in the area around the Rock House, and knew a great deal about it, although he claimed to never have been there. He was able to give a detailed description of the landscape, even mentioning a little spring that flowed through a glade opposite the mouth of the tunnel. The trader had been to the Rock House, but he had never noticed the little spring the Spainard described. He told the Spainard that there was no such spring. Yet, when the trader returned to the place, he found the spring exactly where the Spainard said it would be.

The Spainard told the trader that he was the son of the man that found the silver mine many years before and who had encountered the hunters. The younger Spainard said we was going back to the place and work the mine. He said he could find the mine because his father had left him a hand drawn map and a description of the area.

The story of the second Spaniard continued that his trip to Tennessee was delayed because he developed a case of "fever" and could not leave New Orleans for a considerable amount of time. Perhaps still ill, the Spainard finally made his way to Nashville, but before he could make the trip to the silver mine, he died.

Two Nashvillians took possession of the dead Spainard's belongings. Among his effects, they discovered the description of the area around the Rock House, and the treasure map that the dead man put so much stock in. Duly impressed by the map, the two men decided follow the map and gain the wealth offered by the lost mine.

Accompanied by a guide, the two treasure seekers made their way to where the mine was supposed to be and received permission to "look over the McKinniss Farm." What they saw during their brief survey excited the two Nashvillians. They offered Neil McKinniss half of all the precious metal they found if he would allow them to mine his property.

McKinniss was skeptical of the treasure seekers and despite their promise that they would make him rich beyond his wildest dreams, he denied them the right to mine his farm and sent them on their way. The two disappointed men returned to Nashville with nothing more than the map they had retrieved from the dead Spainard.

Great hidden treasure stories, mythical or not, take on a life of their own and continue for decades, even centuries. Our story continues with the son of Neil McKinniss.

Neil McKinniss died around 1860 and his son. George inherited the Rock House property. George knew the legends about the massive silver lode on his property and he developed a case of silver fever. Not only did he prospect the farm himself, but he allowed others to prospect it as well.

The prospectors procured dynamite and blasted large parts of the farm hoping to uncover the hidden silver mine. They blew massive holes in the hillsides and before they finished, the devastated farm looked as if an earthquake had struck it. One of the prospectors was a man named Donoho. He spent a sizable sum in his quest to find the mythical silver mine, but it avoided him.

In 1905, the property was in the hands of John Sherman Donoho (1865-1959). Donoho had invested a large amount of effort and resources exploring the supposed site of the lost mine and he believed that it was just a matter of time before he uncovered a large vein of silver. That is, if he could get the necessary equipment there to employ "modern methods" to find it. That is where the expansion of the railroad came into play.

The site of the lost mine was believed to be about three miles east of the Willette community wedged in the southeastern corner of Macon County and very near the Jackson County line. The area was as "wild and picturesque" as anywhere in Tennessee. The alleged mine was about 20 miles from the nearest railroad track. But the proposed extension of the line would bring trains within a mere seven miles of the place. It would be much easier and cheaper to get the necessary equipment there from such a short distance than it would be to haul it 20 miles over rough country.

Sadly, for Donoho, the rail line never appeared and he never found the lost mine.

The story above is only one of the many that have been told about Macon County's lost silver mine. Renowned for his ability to make people smile, W. P. Canon came from North Nashville for one of his frequent visits to the hotel in Red Boiling Springs in 1893. Canon had with him a sample of silver ore and an interesting tale as to how he came by it. He said the ore came from a mine in Macon County several years earlier.

According to Canon, a criminal found the mine while he was hiding out in Macon County's rough hills. After the criminal was captured, convicted, and sentenced to life in the Tennessee State Prison, Canon visited him. The convict gave Canon the sample and revealed the location of the mine. Upon testing, the sample revealed a rich silver content and Canon swore he was "pushing preparations for an early development of the mine." Evidently, he never did.

There are also stories of gold in the hills of Tennessee. Oddly, the reports were that the gold was in the same general area as the lost silver mine. In 1899, there was a story about a gold mine being found in Macon County near the Willette community. The alleged gold strike took place on the farms of Joe Livingston and John Shrume (Shrum?). The story went that Shrume had received an enormous offer of $10,000 for his gold-laden farm, but that he turned it down.

The stories of gold continued and in 1905, there were reports that ore taken from near the Rock House assayed at a value of $40 (more than $4,300 in today's currency) of gold per ton. That amounts to about two ounces of gold per ton of ore. It was an exciting development. If there was that degree of gold in the Macon County soil, it would match some of the largest gold bonanzas in history. One area reporter commented, "If all the gold should be gotten from this mine as anticipated, the Republicans and gold Democrats would have a good claim for the single gold standard in the United States."

Alas, there isn't any record of anyone growing rich from mining precious metals in Macon County. However, dreams are sometimes as good as riches.

December 13, 1908. The rumor mill had it that a group of "Chicago capitalists" were leasing property along the border between Tennessee and Kentucky with an eye toward drilling for oil and testing for other minerals. The capitalists were believed to be leasing land near Red Boiling Springs, and would lease property in Monroe County, Kentucky soon. Allegedly, the group from Chicago claimed there was "ample evidence of the existence of oil and minerals to justify" drilling. The wildcatters promised that as soon as they had secured enough leases, and they had the machinery on the ground, they would begin drilling.

It is unknown if these would-be oil men planning to develop the area around Red Boiling Springs were the same collection of "Chicago capitalists" that proposed building a railroad through Red Boiling Springs in 1906.

September 30, 1910. Reports were that oil had been struck in northern Macon County near Red Boiling Springs. The oil was said to be of a "fine amber color and burns very freely." The oil was found 42 feet below "very hard rock." On October 6, G. W. Hunt of Adairville, Kentucky and James Trappe of Tombstone, Arizona secured the option on the "fine oil well" and they stated that they intended to develop it.

November 5, 1912. Workers of the Kensee Oil and Gas Company were boring a well on Long Hungry creek near Red Boiling Springs when they struck a pocket of natural gas about 100 feet below the surface of the ground. The natural gas caused an explosion. According to witnesses, the explosion was heard as far away as six miles away and propelled the 6,000-pound drill 200 to 300 feet into the air. No one was injured in the explosion, but the badly bent drill had to be sent to Nashville for repair.

September 7, 1919. A cartel of "Western oil capitalists" represented by F. W. Eastman of Wichita, Kansas, and several local businessmen took oil options on most of Macon County. They made their headquarters in Red Boiling Springs. Eastman claimed that "after thorough inspections, there is abundant evidence of a paying oil section in this county." The cartel had 90 days to begin boring and other preliminary work or forfeit the options.

6. Other Entertainments

Red Boiling Springs was, and is, about more than just its hotels and waters. The residents of the small town have always found interesting ways to amuse themselves. This chapter explores some of the entertainments the citizens of Red Boiling Springs enjoyed from the beginning of the 20th Century until the end of World War II.

March 2, 1904. Red Boiling Springs residents found many ways to spend their spare time. One favorite activity was joining organizations. A new Odd Fellow lodge was instituted at Red Boiling Springs by W. F. Sander, District Deputy Grand Master of Gainesboro, Tennessee and 22 Charter members. The new lodge was known as Red Boiling Springs Lodge 426. Winfield Scott Poteet was elected Noble Grand of the Lodge, and W. A. Baker was elected Secretary.

September 3, 1906. The director of the Women's Department of the Tennessee State Fair appointed Katheryne McClellan of Red Boiling Springs as one of the committee members from Macon County.

June 15, 1907. It was natural for the Odd Fellows and Masons to work together in common causes. In Red Boiling Springs the Odd Fellows and the Masons combined their resources to build a new meeting hall that they both could use.

July 11, 1911. There was an important meeting of the "Tennessee Snipe Club" held an important meeting at 8 p.m. in the offices of club Secretary Paul D. Denton at 124 East Avenue North in Nashville. The President of Cumberland University Law School, and loyal adviser to the club, addressed the members.

The women members of the club served refreshments.

The purpose of the meeting was to plan the club's first annual convention at its birthplace in Red Boiling Springs. A group of "prominent people of Nashville and other sections of the state" had formed the club at the resort in 1910 and they considered Red Boiling Springs to be the club's Mecca.

There was another meeting on July 18 to continue the planning.

By September 22, the club, now being called "The United Snipe Hunters," was going rapidly, so rapidly that its leaders were considering taking it nationwide. They met at Paul D. Denton's home and elected the following officers: J. V. Kisvar (Grand Hunter); Sol Hyman (Vice Hunter); Paul D. Denton (Scroll Keeper); Thomas Tyler Cloyd (Assistant Scroll Keeper); Mrs. A. C. Bailey (Finance Keeper); C. E. Major (Gate Keeper); and Gun Keepers Lee Wilhoite, Walter Cregar, Paul D. Denton, R. A. Harrington, A. C. Bailey, and Sol Hyman. Cloyd was from Red Boiling Springs. The others were Nashvillians.

Club members approved "handsome emblems" and then J. V. Kisvar delivered an "eloquent" speech admonishing club members to do nothing to bring disgrace to the Snipe Hunters. He then appointed a committee to draw up a constitution and by-laws, and another one to plan a lawn festival on the Tuesday after the conclusion of the State Fair.

August 10, 1907. Katheryne McClellan of Red Boiling Springs was again appointed by the Woman's Department of the State Fair to serve on the committee from Macon County. Red Boiling Springs resident Maude Howser was also appointed to the committee.

July 22, 1911. Drinking alcohol has always been a favorite human pastime. Sometimes drinking leads to major problems. Marlin Maxey of Red Boiling Springs purchased a large amount of whiskey and got very drunk. Then, he spent much of that evening trying to pick a fight with Max Jordan, also of Red Boiling Springs.

Jordan considered Maxey to be a friend of his and he tried to avoid trouble with the drunken man. However, Maxey refused to allow Jordan to dissuade him.

Finally, at about 10:30 p.m., Maxey attacked Jordan because of a cigar wrapper. Given no choice, Jordan acting in self-defense pulled his pistol and shot his friend twice. One round grazed Maxey's forehead and the other hit him in the hip. Thankfully, neither wound proved fatal.

When Maxey sobered up, he admitted that the altercation was his fault, and he refused to press charges against Jordan.

May 25, 1915. The United Snipe Hunters met to plan its fifth anniversary celebration. Members intended to make an excursion to the Red Boiling Springs resort in late July. Several "good speakers" addressed the group and refreshments were served.

The Snipe Hunters, according to their by-laws, were formed at Red Boiling Springs by "prominent men of Tennessee, Kentucky, and Alabama" while they were vacationing at the resort. There were 35 charter members, among them were Red Boiling Springs residents, Minnie Davis, and Bette Neece. The United Snipe Hunter's constitution treated everyone equally, and its stated purposes were charity, morality, and frolic." The organization's colors were red, white, and blue. The background of their official emblem was white, there was an image of the head of a Snipe in the center and in the image of a scroll at the top were the letters "U. S. H."

On June 16, the trustees of the United Snipe Hunters announced that they planned to file papers of incorporation. They also said that several people had expressed interest in joining the group. Interested parties were invited to attend the next meeting in Nashville at 144 8th Avenue North where a "dinner in Snipe Style" would be served.

November 9, 1916. The Odd Fellow Grand Master visited Lodge 426 at Red Boiling Springs for the purpose of conferring with the brethren there about the condition of their lodge.

September 1, 1917. The Mighty Haag Circus came to Red Boiling Springs. It was one of the largest traveling shows in the South. It featured lions, tigers, elephants, and other exotic animals. It also had acrobats, trapeze artists, and clowns. The circus was in town for only one day with shows in the afternoon and evening. The entry fee was 35¢.

February 17, 1924. M. A. Simmons of Nashville's Merchants Hotel had been investing heavily in real estate in Red Boiling Springs and had purchased 75 acres on which he intended to build a new summer resort at the famous watering hole and have it operational by May 1. He said he would use water to produce electricity at his resort. Amusements Simmons planned included developing a five acre lake on the property for boating, fishing, and swimming. A baseball field was under construction, and a pavilion for dancing and roller skating was being erected.

Simmons was also building a summer home on the property and he intended to supervise the resort personally.

February 19, 1924. The Red Boiling Springs basketball team took on the undefeated squad from Lafayette. The boys from Lafayette prevailed 28-13 and pushed their record to 6 wins against no losses.

July 14, 1924. Red Boiling Springs had an outstanding baseball team and they proved it by outslugging the Scottsville, Kentucky squad by a score of 12-9.

October 8, 1925. Vanderbilt University utilized a unique method to get fans to come to the October 10, 1925, football game between the Commodores and Texas. Five airplanes filled with advertising matter and free football tickets rumbled off the runway at the Nashville airport and into the autumn sky. Between them, the planes flew over 27 Middle Tennessee towns "dropping the advertisements with a few tickets sprinkled in." Red Boiling Springs was one of the towns that experienced a shower of tickets raining down. It is unknown how many Red Boiling Springs residences used the gifts that floated down from the sky, but those that did witnessed a good football game. Vandy defeated the Long Horns 14-6.

September 17, 1926. The Mighty Haag Circus put on a grand show at Red Boiling Springs. After delighting the large audience, circus workers took everything down, packed it onto big trucks, and headed toward the next stop.

Soon after leaving Red Boiling Springs, a deadly accident occurred. The massive, six-wheel truck carrying the main tent and poles failed to maneuver a steep curve near Hermitage Springs, ran off the road and overturned. Harvey Hall was killed and another circus employee was injured.

Hall was believed to be from West Virginia, but his next of kin couldn't be located and he was buried just across the Tennessee border at Boles, Kentucky.

June 16, 1927. Manager Chester Davis was actively seeking opponents to fill openings in the Red Boiling Springs baseball team's Saturday and Sunday schedules. Apparently, the team would take on all comers.

July 4, 1927. There was an all-day signing at Simmons Lake in Red Boiling Springs. Hundreds of people attended.

July 30, 1927. M. A. Simmons sponsored a boxing card at his Red Boiling Springs amusement park. Beginning at 8:30 p.m. Gene Swan of Nashville took on Jack O'Brien of Louisville in a scheduled 8 round match. In a Bantamweight bout, Young Stafford of Memphis fought a scheduled six rounder with Kid Glasser. Then, Nashville welterweight Bob Sledd engaged in a 4 round slugfest with Nashville's Red Kilgore.

August 5, 1927. The Red Boiling Springs baseball team had a home game against the nine from Scottsville, Kentucky. Red Boiling Springs prevailed 7-6.

The Red Boiling Spring Springs squad was seeking an opponent for August 14.

August 6, 1927. A gun club was formed in Red Boiling Springs. The 25 charter members elected the following officers: Dr. F. B. Clark, President; George Gaines, Vice President; C. Davis, Secretary/Treasurer; and Melvin Miller, Field Captain.

August 26, 1927. The Red Boiling Springs Athletic Club put on another boxing show a mere three weeks after the previous one. Beginning at 8:30 p. m., the event offered as many as 28 rounds of pugilistic excitement. The card featured Chicago's Bill Sullivan against Jack Alden of Cincinnati in an eight round contest. Soldier Milligan of Cowan, Tennessee fought Chiggas Butin of Portland, Tennessee for eight rounds. Nashvillians Kid Coleman and Battling Swan duked it out in a scheduled six rounder. Then, two local boys from Red Boiling Springs, Red Hillgot and Dan Smith entered the square circle and participated in the sweet science for six rounds.

August 18, 1928. The Smith County Fair at Carthage drew visitors from across the Upper Cumberland region. Along with other attractions an eight piece brass band from Red Boiling Springs performed afternoon and evening concerts.

October 8, 1928. The Tennessee Fox Hunters Association began its seventh annual foxhunt trial at daybreak at Red Boiling Springs. The fox hunters were registered at the Palace Hotel where Henry Counts made "special arrangements" for their comfort.

There was a lot involved in a fox hunt. There were about 100 mounted hunters and 7 judges taking part along with about 50 hounds. Nashville fox hunters sent 10 horses to Red Boiling Springs on October 6.

The trial hunt began about eight miles from the Palace Hotel. Two foxes were jumped quickly and they led the hunters on a chase for several miles through the wilderness of eastern Macon

County. The official hunt continued for three days from October 11-13.

September 16, 1930. The Tennessee State Fair was underway in Nashville. As always, livestock breeders from across the state brought prize specimens to be judged. Among them was Dr. Royal A. Leslie of Red Boiling Springs.

February 25, 1932. School sports, especially basketball, have always been popular in Red Boiling Springs. Naturally, some of those teams have been better than others. The Red Boiling Springs boys team took on the Carthage team at Cookeville in the Tennessee Secondary School Athletic Association (TSSAA) District basketball tournament. Carthage won by the lopsided score of 58-7.

September 5, 1932. About 500 people attended a Labor Day Picnic at Red Boiling Springs. The picnic was sponsored by the Red Boiling Post of the American Legion. An old-fashioned barbecue and music performed by the Red Boiling Springs brass band highlighted the event. Congressman John Ridley Mitchell addressed the crowd and spoke in favor of enacting federal legislature to benefit veterans.

February 28, 1934. The Red Boiling Springs basketball team took on the team from Sparta in the TSSAA 10th District tournament. The Sparta five was one of most powerful teams in the state and they overwhelmed Red Boiling Springs 72 to 17.

January 11, 1935. There was an overflow crowd at Nashville's YMCA auditorium to watch a series of amateur boxing matches. In fact, several unlucky boxing enthusiasts were turned away because the auditorium could not seat them.

One of the best fights of the night was a featherweight bout between Nashville's Felix Stevens and Roger "Kid" Kennedy of Red Boiling Springs. Stevens, the 1934 Nashville area Golden Gloves runner-up took a close decision. Observers said Kennedy showed promise and opined that he'd become a "topnotcher." Stevens likely won only because of his advantages in reach and experience.

In another outstanding fight, the "Red Boiling Springs Glove Slinger," lightweight Charles Sabens lost by technical knockout in the waning seconds of the second round to the more experienced Bobby Sanders. Observers said the pugilists "mixed up at close quarters then turned on the steam at long range."

Both Kennedy and Sabens were unsponsored and paid their own expenses to compete in the event.

January 21, 1935. At the Nashville YMCA put on another boxing card. Bobby Sanders knocked out Ray Chitwood of Red Boiling Springs in the second round. In another bout, flyweight Reed Hudson of Red Boiling Springs claimed a decision over Nashville's Jack Witt in an entertaining contest.

February 11, 1935. More than 220 amateur boxers competed in the third annual Golden Gloves boxing tournament sponsored by the Nashville Tennessean. Tournament winners qualified to compete in the national Golden Gloves tournament in Chicago. The tournament was a big event. It proved to have the biggest turnout in tournament history up to that point. 750 ringside seats sold for $2 each.

Boxers from Red Boiling who took part were Roger Kennedy (featherweight), Reed Hudson (flyweight), Ray Chitwood (lightweight), and Charles Sabens (lightweight). The Red Boiling Springs boxers fought hard but none of them advanced to the national tournament.

June 4, 1935. Newspapers have always been an important outlet of information and entertainment for readers in rural America. In mid-1935, Red Boiling Springs had a new weekly newspaper, *The Red Boiling Springs News.* Knox Pitts, a Tennessean by birth who had lived most of his life in Georgia, was the editor. Associate editors were Herman Campbell and Roy Pendleton. The subscription rate was $1.50 per year (50¢ more per year than a subscription to the *Macon County Times*). The *News* was scheduled to be issued each Friday, but the first issue was available to the public on Tuesday, June 4.

July 4, 1935. Amateur boxing was gaining in popularity in Macon County. On Independence Day, American Legion Post No. 117 sponsored a boxing card in Lafayette. In the first bout of the evening, Charles Sabens, the "Red Boiling Springs Glove Slinger," outclassed Tommy Gross of Lafayette and won an easy decision. Gross didn't land a solid blow in the contest, but he was game and he made it to the final bell.

In another bout on the card, "Bearcat" Wooten of Lafayette won a close decision over Ray Chitwood.

"Bug" Howser of Lafayette was the top performer at the event.

Former Macon County Sheriff Virgil Frye promoted the matches with an eye toward putting together a boxing team to represent Macon County in the 1936 Golden Gloves tournament at Nashville.

August 3, 1935. Vernon M. Spivey, singer and evangelist from Chicago, conducted the first of his several religious meetings hosted by the Red Boiling Springs Church of Christ.

September 2, 1935. There was an "All-Day Affair" at the lake in West Red Boiling Springs on Labor Day. The main attraction was popular country music star and Grand Ole Opry performer, Robert Lunn. Lunn and his Nighthawks played dance music for the huge crowd. Lunn, who often performed with country music legend Roy Acuff, became famous for his humorous song, "Talkin' Blues." Other activities offered at the event included boating, picnics, and various games. The person with the day's top bowling score received a prize.

September 2, 1935. Leonard Cave isn't technically in Red Boiling Springs, but it may as well be. On Labor Day 1935, there was an "Old Time Barbecue" held at the cave, followed by afternoon and evening dances. Many Red Boiling Springs residents attended.

March 5, 1936. The pairings were set for the TSSAA 10th District basketball tournament at Cookeville. Red Boiling Springs received a bye in the first round, but in the second round, the boys lost to the Monterey team 34-16.

December 14, 1936. The Knights of Columbus sponsored an amateur boxing event at Nashville's Hippodrome Center. Twelve bouts were on the card and several Red Boiling Springs boxers took part. Roger "Kid" Kennedy knocked out Frank Ballenger of DuPont in the first round. Welterweight Ray Chitwood took a decision from Herbert Robinson of Dickson. Ben Fulghum fought to a draw with Elmer Newsome of DuPont. The "Red Boiling Springs Glove Slinger," Charles Sabens was scheduled to fight a boxer from Trezevant, Tennessee and Terry Moore was supposed to mix it up with a DuPont boxer, but those fights didn't take place.

February 25, 1937. The 10th District Junior High School basketball tournament got underway at Liberty, Tennessee. The Red Boiling Springs girls team lost in the first round to La Guardo 13-3. The boys from Red Boiling Springs received a first round bye then lost in the second round to Fourth Model in a closely contested battle 29-24.

More serious than losing basketball games, some of the boys from Red Boiling Springs were exposed to measles and they brought the disease back home with them. Soon, there was a widespread outbreak of measles in the town. The good news was that when the school term ended, the spread of measles among students ended, and the epidemic ceased.

April 23, 1937. *The Red Boiling Springs News* ceased publication. The newspaper had struggled throughout its existence to find an audience and it could not justify continuing.

But the editors stated that production was merely suspended and there was hope that the paper might be revived in the future.

For some time, the *News* had been printed in Gainesboro, Tennessee by the *Sentinel* under the direction of publishers Fred L. Tardy and Burnley G. Cassetty. Cordell Parkhurst ran the Red Boiling side of the operation. When the paper folded, Parkhurst immediately received another job offer, but he didn't accept it right away.

March 26, 1938. Red Boiling Springs sent representatives to the tenth annual Fifth District Interscholastic Literary League meet at Cookeville on the campus of Tennessee Polytechnic Institute (now Tennessee Tech). 135 students from across the region, both male and female, took part in various literary competitions including debating, declamation, original oratory, extemporaneous speaking, one-act plays, and humorous and dramatic readings. Institute faculty judged the competitors.

August 20, 1938. Parks are important places of recreation in most cities. Parks have always mattered to Red Boiling Springs. They mattered especially to Red Boiling Springs resident Thomas Jefferson Wooten.

As a young man, Wooten planted ginseng and goldenseal gardens in a small nursery. The produce from these gardens became famous throughout the United States and made Wooten prosperous. Financially secure, Wooten began concentrating on building and developing Wooten Park in Red Boiling Springs. Although he had not seen his vision for the park fully realized when he died on August 20, 1938, at the age of 71, the park had progressed to the point that thousands of people visited it annually.

September 17, 1938. Drinking establishments serve as places of recreation virtually everywhere. There were, and are, many bars surrounding Red Boiling Springs. Then, as now, some bars are "rough joints." One such place was the Hill Top Inn near Hermitage Springs in Clay County, Tennessee. Around midnight on September 17, 1938, a brawl broke out there and the proprietor, Esty Woods tried to stop it. As the melee continued, Estes Browning of Red Boiling Springs drew his .32-caliber pistol, and he fired it twice. Both bullets struck Woods in the abdomen, wounding him fatally. Woods expired about an hour later, and the authorities took Browning into custody.

January 3, 1939. The TSSAA awarded hosting privileges for the 18th District Basketball Tournament to Celina. Celina had a new gymnasium which made it a natural place to host the tourney. 13 teams were invited to compete, including the Red Boiling Springs five.

In the first round of the tournament on March 2, Red Boiling Springs defeated Clark Range 32-26. In the quarterfinals the next day, Red Boiling Springs fell to Gainesboro 49-27.

January 31, 1939. Bantamweight (118 pounds) Noel McLerran was one of two boxers from Red Boiling Springs to take part in the seventh annual Golden Gloves Tournament in Nashville. The 1939 tourney was held at Ryman Auditorium and boxers from 37 towns took part. McLerran fought in the novice division.

February 25, 1939. There was a formal foxhunt at Red Boiling Springs. The hunters in their traditional crimson colored English garb, mounted their steeds. The hounds shattered the serenity of the early winter's morning with their louds barks. The clever fox avoided its pursuers as it led them on a romp of several miles. The scene was repeated every morning for a week.

The area was well-suited for foxhunts. The Master of the Hunt stated, "Between Red Boiling Springs and Fountain Run, Kentucky is one of the few areas of the United States where the fencing is rail instead of wire. There are 10 or 15 miles of it making an ideal foxhunting country." Jumping wire fences was much more dangerous for horses than rail fences were. For one thing, the horses and riders could see rail fences before they could see wire fences and they could prepare for jumps sooner.

There was a push underway to make Red Boiling Springs the permanent site of the National Foxhunters Association field trials. If Red Boiling Springs became the home of the trials, it would be boost to Tennessee in the sports community and would benefit the state and local economy as well.

March 23, 1939. As part of their three-day tour of mid-state towns, the David Lipscomb College Quartet performed at Red Boiling Springs.

January 21, 1940. Noel McLerran, age 17, was again entered in the Golden Gloves boxing tournament. In 1940, he fought in the flyweight (112 pound) division.

McLerran was soon engaged in a tougher fight. Entering the service during World War II, on December 16, 1944, Private McLerran was killed during the battle of Leyte in the Philippines.

February 29, 1940. In the 18th District TSSAA basketball tournament, Hilman defeated Red Boiling Springs girls 36-24.

January 30, 1941. Loyal D. Maynard, a Red Boiling Springs heavyweight, was scheduled to fight Owen Casey of the Elks Club team in the Golden Gloves boxing tournament at Nashville. Maynard lost by forfeit.

January 15, 1942. The basketball season was underway. Red Boiling Springs high school had strong teams, but they also had very tough schedules. Some of their scores that season included:

January 15: The Red Boiling Springs boys defeated Macon County High 50-35; the girls lost to the team from Lafayette 33-25.

January 17: The boys traveled to Nashville and lost to David Lipscomb High 47-27.

January 24, 1942: The boys lost to Lebanon 35-25; the girls lost to Lebanon 38-23.

February 25, 1942: In the TSSAA District tourney, the Red Boiling Springs girls lost to Westmoreland 50-17.

November 25, 1942. The David Lipscomb College basketball team opened its season. William Meador of Red Boiling Springs was a member of the team. He played guard.

February 20, 1945. The Red Boiling Springs girls team fell to the Trousdale County five 20-16 in the TSSAA District 9 basketball Tournament.

7. Education

Education is important in every community, and Red Boiling Springs was no different than any other town. This chapter looks at some of the educational activities in Red Boiling Springs and details some things about the students that came from the town.

July 30, 1905. It appeared that Red Boiling Springs was getting a new prep school. The project was under the supervision of the Methodist Episcopal Church and the local members of the Board of Trustees were actively involved in building the structure. The two-story 60' by 40' wooden schoolhouse would have rooms that were "high, airy, light, and pleasant." 80,000 board feet of lumber would be used to build it.

Construction of the Red Boiling Springs "College" was reportedly "well in hand." The doors, windows, and fixtures had been ordered and received at Carthage before the middle of June. A special committee was appointed to select and purchase the roofing material. The expectation was that the roof would be on and the schoolhouse weatherboarded by September 1. Builders could then continue their work, regardless of the weather.

Building the school would not come cheaply. The estimated cost was $4,500 (more than $160,000 today) of which $1,500 was still needed to finish it. The Trustees for the project in Nashville, W. J. O'Callaghan, and R. Pierce (who was also the Financial Agent for the project) hoped the people of the city would kick in $1,000 toward the completion of the building. Pierce said, "Many of our people go to this pleasant summer resort. All that country trades with Nashville. If anyone can point out a location where a classical school – an academic and collegiate institution combined – is more needed and where there is a larger and more inviting field of usefulness, please do."

One could send their donations to the Nashville post office in the care of O'Callahan, or to Pierce at 107 29th Avenue, Nashville. The two men would forward the money they received to the group's Treasurer at Red Boiling Springs, L. S. York.

The plan was to finish and dedicate the no later than October or November. Bishop Luther B. Wilson of Chattanooga, W. P. Thrikfeld of Cincinnati, and several faculty members of Grant University were to participate in the dedication. The hope was that classes would commence no later than January 1, 1906.

September 8, 1907. The private academy in Red Boiling Springs called Welsey Memorial College (referred to as Weslyn College by some sources) was headed by A. M. Keels. Mable Howser was one of the teachers. The academy ceased to be a preparatory school around 1912 but continued as a "common" school for several years after that.

February 3, 1909. Several leaders in Red Boiling Springs felt placing their town in its own special school district would aid education in eastern Macon County. Upon receiving the petition from the group, Tennessee State Senator James T. Baskerville of Gallatin introduced a bill creating the special district.

August 24, 1910. Virginia P. Moore, the state organizer of the Tennessee School Improvement Association was in Red Boiling Springs organizing the Macon County association. The officers of the Macon County organization were D. Henry Piper of Lafayette (President), Nelle Simmons of Lafayette (Vice President), O. D. Davis of Hillsdale (Treasurer), and Eliza Bridwell of Red Boiling Springs (Secretary).

June 19, 1922. A "teachers' institute and educational Chautauqua for the teachers of the counties of Macon, Clay, Jackson, Smith, Robertson, Trousdale, and Sumner" opened at Red Boiling Springs. The meetings that continued through June 29 offered "splendid programs for both the institute and the Chautauqua."

Chautauqua was an adult education and social movement in the United States. Chautauqua brought entertainment and culture for the whole community, with speakers, teachers, musicians, showmen, preachers, and specialists of the day. President Theodore Roosevelt is often quoted as saying that Chautauqua was "the most American thing in America."

Attendees of the institute at Red Boiling Springs said it was the best ever held. The large pavilion at the Donoho Hotel where the meetings were held overflowed with teachers, citizens of Red Boiling Springs, and visitors from across the area.

County School Board members conducted morning and afternoon sessions. The former Tennessee State Superintendent of schools taught institute participants in the "primary methods" of educating students and gave daily lectures and demonstrations in spelling and reading.

On the morning of June 22, Dr. Harry Clark addressed the teachers and others at the Chautauqua on "The Necessity of Developing our Talent." On the evening of June 23, Dr. R. K. Morgan gave his audience a "good practical sermon." On the afternoon of June 24, Professor John W. Williams of Portland, Tennessee addressed a large audience on the subject of "Masonry."

The proprietor of the Donoho Hotel invited the teachers to return for their annual Institute in 1923.

June 18, 1923. Another teachers' institute and educational Chautauqua opened in Red Boiling Springs. The 1923 event continued for ten days. Speakers at the event included N. T. Lowery, J. W. Brister, and Dr. Harry Clark, of Nashville; T. J. Durham of Gallatin; J. B. Brown of Chattanooga; R. A. Lynn of Murfreesboro; A. W. Smith and Q. M. Smith of Cookeville; Drs. J. R. Hobbs and J. T. McNew of Brimingham, Alabama; and Tennessee Commissioner of Education, P. L. Harned.

Those involved said the event was "one of the best institutes ever held in the state." The attendance was large and observers commented that "The best educators and talent in the state are employed and no expense or trouble has been spared in giving the teachers and through them the children the very best that's to be had."

Education Commissioner P. L. Harned played a major role in the event. He presided over the executive session of the county superintendents and county school board members. On June 27 he addressed the assembly on the "problems which confront teachers of Tennessee.

June 22, 1924. At Red Boiling Springs a Teachers' Institute and Educational Chautauqua opened. The third annual affair lasted until June 29. The meeting sported a greater attendance than the previous two. Teachers from Macon, Trousdale, Sumner, Clay, Smith, and Jackson counties participated. Part of the reason that more teachers made reservations at the week-long affair was that Red Boiling Springs hotels were offered them reduced rates. The Louisville & Nashville Railroad offered reduced rates to the teachers too.

Speakers at the event included State Senator James T. Baskerville, Drs. George A., and R. T. Morgan, J. B. Brown, and President of the State Teachers' Association John W. Williams.

In 1925, the Teachers' Institute and Educational Chautauqua moved to Epperson Springs in western Macon County.

October 11, 1926. There was a desperate need for improved education in Macon County. The white illiteracy rate countywide stood at 22% which meant that Macon had the second lowest literacy rate in Tennessee. Yet, there was not a first-class, four-year high school in the county. For years, efforts to build a new high school had come to nothing. Finally, in 1925, the Tennessee legislature voted to compel every county in the state to have at least one accredited four-year high school. After a court battle that ended with the legislative act being upheld, the Macon County Court (legislative body) began the process of building a new school.

The County Court voted to allocate $12,000 toward the new building and opened bids to any town or community desirous of having the new school within its confines. The County Court stipulated that all bids had to be at least $5,000. Three bids were entered. Lafayette and the Galen Community placed bids of $5,000 each and Red Boiling Springs bid $12,000. When all the bids were in, community leaders in Galen requested that their bid be withdrawn in favor of Lafayette.

The final decision was left to the Macon County School Board which, despite the higher bid from Red Boiling Springs, voted 5-1 in favor of accepting Lafayette's bid. Donnie Bennett was the only board member to vote for building the school at Red Boiling Springs.

June 23, 1927. An educational and good roads conference for the fourth congression district opened at Red Boiling Springs. The conference ran until June 26. State Education Commissioner P. L. Harned and State Schools Inspector W.A. Bass were present as was W. K. Sharp Jr. of the Tennessee State Health Department.

Harned told those attending the conference that standardization had improved education in Tennessee. Several area speakers also made presentations.

July 28, 1927. A 10 a.m. blaze destroyed the Red Boiling Springs school. The wooden building went up quickly and nothing could be saved. The school's contents including laboratory equipment and a piano were lost. The timing of the fire could hardly have been worse. The fall term was scheduled to begin on August 1.

Arson was suspected and bloodhounds were brought in, but they didn't find a trail to followed.

Undeterred by the loss of the school, classes got underway in Red Boiling Springs in late September. Professor C. W. Davis served as the principal to more than 20 junior high schoolers and Lena Birdwell taught 27 seventh and eighth graders at the local Masonic Lodge. J. L. Hawkins taught 37 fifth and sixth graders at the Presbyterian Church. Vera York acted at the teacher for about 50 third and fourth graders and Erma York taught 66 first and second graders at the Christian Church. Later, some of the fourth graders were transferred to the Presbyterian Church.

Tables, chairs, lockers, and blackboards were provided by local citizens and donations were taken to purchase new playground equipment.

School authorities were pleased that at least 90% of the student body had been inoculated for typhoid and diphtheria.

May 2, 1928. The places used as replacement schools in Red Boiling Springs after the fire in 1927 worked in a pinch, but they weren't a long-term solution. A new school was needed and the Macon County Court levied a tax to help build it. The Macon County Board of Education also set aside a sum to aid in the building project. The citizens of Red Boiling Springs did their part by pledging money for the school. The hope was that the new schoolhouse would be ready in time for the upcoming school year.

May 24, 1929. The school year in Red Boiling Springs ended. The town didn't have a four-year high school, but 24 students had attended junior high school classes, 13 of which were graduating sophomores. The sophomores received certificates that allowed them to continue their studies at a four-year high school that fall.

April 27, 1931. The Parent-Teacher Convention of the 7th District opened at Red Boiling Springs. Delegates from several counties attended.

August 6, 1934. Schools across Macon County opened. At the Junior High School at Red Boiling Springs Victor Keen served as principal and the teachers were Dulcie McDonald, Eva Butrum, Mattie Jenkins, Geneva Witcher, Coby Lee Kirby, and Anna Chitwood.

June 18, 1936. Those selected to serve at the Red Boiling Springs Junior High School were Principal C. W. Davis and teachers Dulcie McDonald, Hattie Jenkins, Colby Lee Kirby, Elizabeth Chitwood, Anna Chitwood, Eva Butrum Chitwood, and Freeman Crowder.

April 5, 1937. All 27 magistrates were present at the meeting of the Macon County Court. One important matter of discussion was a request for an appropriation to establish a four-year high school at Red Boiling Springs. At the time, Red Boiling Springs only had a junior high school. The County Court was expected to appropriate the necessary funds at its next meeting.

April 29, 1937. The Macon County Board of Education chose teachers for the upcoming school year. C.W. Davis was again named principal of Red Boiling Springs High. Those chosen to teach at Red Boiling Springs Elementary were Hattie Jenkins, Elizabeth Chitwood, Anna Chitwood, Eva Chitwood, and Geneva Kemp.

June 28, 1940. Students from seven states were enrolled in summer classes at Lebanon Tennessee's Cumberland University. A few Red Boiling Springs residents were among those attending classes there.

August 24, 1940. Herman Taylor, the principal of Red Boiling Springs elementary and high school reported a total enrollment of 391 pupils, 104 of which were attending high school. The high school class officers were:

Seniors: Mildred Dycus (President); Fred Russell (Vice President); Elma Crowder (Secretary); Cornelia Ramsey (Treasurer).

Juniors: Flo Jenkins (President); Perry D. Compton (Vice President); Alma June Smith (Secretary); Bernice Davis (Treasurer).

Sophomores: Georgia Patterson (President); Freda Parkhurst (Vice President); R. Parkhurst (Secretary); Ruth Carter (Treasurer).

Freshmen: Willis Clark (President); Lucille Craighead (Vice President); Clay Gaines (Secretary); Benard Parkhurst (Treasurer).

May 8, 1941. The faculty of Red Boiling Springs High School announced that Wynema Copas, the daughter of Hillas and Ola Copas was school valedictorian. Helen Spivey, the daughter of Rad and Ollie Spivey was Salutatorian.

May 2, 1943. Jean Compton and Fay Joines of Red Boiling Springs were graduating from high school. In their entire twelve years of education, neither had ever missed a day of classes.

October 14, 1944. There was an outbreak of scarlet fever in Macon County. In the northeastern corner of Macon County, officials closed the school at the Sunrise community until the danger from the disease passed. Other communities affected by scarlet fever included Red Boiling Springs, Bellevue, and Galen, but schools were not closed in those places.

8. Politicians Visit Red Boiling Springs

Over the years, several politicians came to Red Boiling Springs to either vacation or to campaign there. Being a first-class resort, Red Boiling Springs attracted several well-heeled politicians desiring rest and relaxation. Beyond that, despite its small population, Red Boiling Springs was a prime destination for candidates. The reason for this was that the guests at the hotel included a large number of political movers and shakers and their support was vital to a successful campaign. This chapter relates the activities of some of the politicians, famous and not, that visited Red Boiling Springs in the first half of the 20th Century.

August 4, 1900. Judge J. Mack Anderson left Nashville on his way to Red Boiling Springs.

August 13, 1902. United States Representative Rice A. Pierce had to cut short his vacation at Red Boiling Springs to go to Ashville, North Carolina and attend to his ill son. He returned to Red Boiling Springs later and remained until September 8.

August 4, 1904. Charles Myers, Assistant City Treasurer of Nashville went to Red Boiling Springs "on account of his health." He intended to stay at the resort for "about a month."

August 28, 1904. Nashville City Attorney Kinnard Taylor McConnico was on holiday at Red Boiling Springs, but his work got in the way. He had to attend pressing business in Nashville. He was able to handle his work via the mail and he did not have to leave cool and shady Red Boiling Springs prematurely.

July 22, 1906. Chief Justice of the Tennessee Supreme Court, William Dwight Beard, and his spouse had travelled from

Memphis to vacation at Red Boiling Springs. They returned home on July 31.

July 28, 1906. Judge Levi S. Woods of Henderson, Kentucky was headed to Red Boiling Springs for a stay of two weeks.

June 22, 1907. Tennessee State Comptroller, Frank Dibrell made his way to Red Boiling Springs to "recuperate for about two weeks." Dibrell returned to Nashville on July 6, and went back to work on July 8. He reported that he was "very much pleased with his trip" and that he was "very much recuperated."

July 27, 1907. Tennessee Secretary of State, John W. Morton, had been on a "summer outing" at Red Boiling Springs for several weeks. He was enjoying himself, but there was mounting pressure on him to return to his duties and chair a meeting of the Tennessee Board of Equalization. The most important matter facing the board was to determine if 20,000 acres of Tennessee mountain land belonged in Bledsoe or Sequatchie County.

Morton returned to Nashville on August 1 and the board met on August 5.

July 1, 1908. Tennessee Secretary of State, John W. Morton, was very ill. He had been in Red Boiling Springs for some time trying to recover. However, Moore had to pull himself from his sickbed on July 2 and return to Nashville to be with his son, John W. Morton, Jr. The younger Morton was at St. Thomas Hospital undergoing an appendicitis operation. The operation went well, and the elder Morton returned to Red Boiling Springs a few days later.

The younger Morton returned to work on August 8.

On August 14, the Secretary of State said he "was rapidly improving now." He said he expected to be back at work soon. Morton reassumed his duties on August 17. He was "looking and feeling well" and he reported that "the stay at the springs benefitted him very much."

July 17, 1908. Tennessee Supreme Court Justice William K. McAlister and his spouse, Laura, went to Red Boiling Springs for a vacation. They returned on September 7.

Justice Alister's son, Hill, later became Governor of Tennessee.

July 27, 1908. West Tennessee political operative, W. W. Baird of Humboldt was on his way home after a vacation of two weeks at Red Boiling Springs. Baird was working for Governor Malcomb R. Patterson's reelection. Baird was certain that Patterson would win reelection. The election was close, but Patterson did win.

August 18, 1908. Nashville City Judge Baker returned from his one week outing at Red Boiling Springs. It was a good thing that Baker was in "fine spirits," because more than 100 cases "confronted" him when he reopened his court.

August 26, 1908. Recently prevailing in the election for Davidson County Sheriff, Samuel Houston Borum was taking a rest at Red Boiling before assuming office in September. It was a working vacation as Borum was using his time away from the distractions of Nashville to consider the many applications he had received from those wishing to become deputies.

September 20, 1908. William B. Brewer, the editor of the *Fairview Review* of Farview, Kentucky, suffered a stroke that left him partially paralyzed. He had just returned from Red Boiling Springs where he had been seeking relief from his kidney disease. In the previous election, Brewer had narrowly lost a bid to represent Todd County in the Kentucky legislature.

May 31, 1909. State Representative F. G. Buford of Giles County was one of the most powerful members of the Tennessee legislature. However, he was suffering through "a long illness." He went to Red Boiling Springs for a few weeks to recuperate.

July 1, 1909. Laura McAlister, the spouse of Tennessee Supreme Court Justice, William K. McAlister, and Martha Dickinson, the

144

spouse of former Tennessee Supreme Court Justice, Jacob M. Dickinson, were close friends. The two women were planning a vacation to Red Boiling Springs.

July 23, 1909. Davidson County Sheriff Sam Houston Borum was taking his annual vacation at Red Boiling Springs. His spouse Mary and their sons Vernon and Chester were with him.

The Sheriff's stay went longer than he had planned, and he was sure to have wished that he had departed sooner. On August 8, Vernon Borum who was mere days short of turning 14, engaged in an altercation with an African American lad of about the same age. Angry, Vernon picked up a rock intending to strike his opponent, but a bystander took the rock from the boy before he could hurl it.

Sheriff Borum, who had witnessed the entire event, resented the fact that his son was prevented from clobbering the other youth. The Sheriff engaged in a heated argument with the would-be peacemaker who was much smaller than he was. Finally, the threatening Sheriff demanded the rock and the Good Samaritan let him have it.

In a David and Goliath type scene, the man that had tried to prevent the boys from fighting, threw the rock as hard as he could, and it struck the angry Sheriff in the face. Borum staggered and would have fallen to the ground, but a friend caught him before he did.

August 27, 1909. Andrew McClellan of Dickson, Tennessee was headed home after a vacation in Red Boiling of several weeks. McClellan wanted to rest before he embarked upon a campaign to recapture the seat in the state legislature that he had held a few years before.

September 18, 1909. Judge Philip Lindsey was on vacation at Red Boiling Springs. Lindsey had been the President of the Nashville City Council and a member of the Tennessee legislature before moving to Texas where he practiced law and penned several books.

August 2, 1910. There was a split in the Tennessee Democratic Party. The were allegations that Governor Malcom R. Patterson was trying to control the state's judiciary and he was opposed by citizens of both political parties. During an anti-Patterson rally at Red Boiling Springs, W. D. Houser of Clarksville, and Macon County attorney W. A. Smith gave stirring speeches.

The split among the Democrats made Patterson unelectable and he dropped out of the race. The Democrats then turned to former Governor and sitting US Senator Robert Love Taylor. However, Taylor lost a very close General Election contest to Republican Ben W. Hooper.

August 23, 1910. Chris Kreis, Deputy Davidson County Court Clerk; Davidson County Grand Jury Officer W. T. Jones; and Reed Strong left Nashville for a stay at Red Boiling Springs for about 10 days.

August 26, 1910. Hill McAlister and his spouse Louise returned home from a vacation at Red Boiling Springs. McAlister had served as Nashville City Attorney and was elected to the State Senate in 1910. He served as Tennessee Governor from 1933 to 1937.

September 3, 1910. State Senator A. A. Matthews returned to Nashville after a month-long rest at Red Boiling Springs.

October 19, 1911. Tennessee State Railroad Commissioner Frank Avent, and his spouse Mayne, went on vacation at Red Boiling Springs. They returned home on November 4.

August 21, 1914. Tennessee Supreme Court Justice Dick Latta Lansden of Cookeville was at Red Boiling Springs recuperating. Lansden had been in a "precarious state of health for several weeks." His condition "was a source of deep anxiety to his friends throughout the state." Judge Lansden recovered rapidly and returned to work. He became Chief Justice of the Tennessee High Court in 1918.

August 24, 1914. Davidson County Court Clerk Will F. Hunt had started a vacation at Red Boiling Springs.

August 12, 1917. Mrs. L. F. Butler, the President of the Political Study Club of the Tennessee Equal Suffrage Association, returned to Nashville after several weeks at Red Boiling Springs. An avid driver, Butler had been involved in a crash in Nashville and was seriously injured. After recuperating in Red Boiling Springs, she said she was almost completely recovered.

August 14, 1917. Tennessee State Senator Moses H. Allen of Lafayette sent a reminder to the members of the previous General Assembly:

"To the members of the sixtieth General Assembly of the state of Tennessee –

"Gentlemen: You Remember at the close of the last general assembly that I introduced and had passed a resolution inviting the members of the senate to meet at Red Boiling Springs on August 15, 1917, for a reunion for all members, clerks, attaches, etc., also the third house? I went over to the house and my good friend, G. A. Marcan, of Shelby County, introduced and had passed unanimously a like resolution, which invitation was heartily accepted by both houses, with the assurance that all members, clerks, etc., attend the reunion on the above date. Now this reminder is for you to get ready and be at Red Boiling Springs on August 15, 1917, so that we may renew our acquaintance, friendship and love for one another. Plenty of good hotels and the best water in the Southland."

April 6, 1918. L. G. Boxwell and Z. D. Dunlap spoke at a community meeting at Red Boiling Springs. The purpose of the meeting was to increase interest in purchasing Liberty Bonds.

Boxwell and Dunlap were "four-minute men." Four-minute men were volunteers authorized by President Wilson to spread pro-administration propaganda. Their speeches were derived from talking points provided by the Committee of Information in Washington.

Liberty Bonds were sold in 1917 and 1918 to help finance the Allied effort in World War I.

July 22, 1918. Tennessee State Senator Cicero Dowlen ended his reelection bid and withdrew from the contest. Dowlen was in declining health and soon after his withdrawal, he traveled to Red Boiling Springs to recuperate.

August 3, 1919. E. M. Perkins, the Mayor of Franklin, Tennessee spent several weeks at Red Boiling Springs. Upon his return home, Perkins said that he was "greatly improved in health." Despite his rejuvenation, Perkins declined to stand for reelection.

October 2, 1920. Republican nominee for Governor, Alfred A. Taylor, campaigned at Red Boiling Springs. That November, Taylor defeated incumbent Governor Albert H. Roberts.

October 18, 1920. Republican nominee for Congress, Wynne F. Clouse, campaigned at Red Boiling Springs. Clouse defeated incumbent Cordell Hull in the General Election.

June 24, 1921. Tennessee Secretary of State, Ernest N. Haston, was on vacation at Red Boiling Springs. He expected to stay there for a few weeks.

June 27, 1922. Democratic candidate for Tennessee Governor, Austin Peay campaigned during the Chautauqua taking place at Red Boiling Springs. About 150 "teachers and farmers" listened to the speech. Peay won a close primary contest, and then prevailed in the General Election by a wider margin.

August 21, 1922. Fred Sheperd, a political operative for the Democratic Party from Chattanooga had just wrapped up a stay of one week at Red Boiling Springs. Sheperd stated that despite the fact that "up in Macon County around Red Boiling Springs" there were a lot of Republicans, the Democratic nominee Austin Peay would get a large bloc of votes. Sheperd was right in a way.

In Macon County, the Democratic vote in the Governor's race was 242 votes lower than it had been in 1920, but the Democratic percentage in Macon County rose to 33.4% from 24.1% in the previous election.

October 28, 1922. Governor Alfred Taylor was in an uphill reelection battle, but he was fighting. At noon on October 28, the Governor gave a formal speech at Red Boiling Springs. While most Red Boiling Springs voters liked Taylor, he didn't excite them and they didn't hurry to the polls to vote for him.

Soon after Taylor departed, Cordell Hull arrived and gave his own speech to more than 400 men and women. Hull, a Democrat, was trying to regain the congressional seat he lost in the previous election. Hull won the election easily.

September 17, 1924. Gibson County, Tennessee Trustee, J. E. Mays, left his West Tennessee home on his way to Red Boiling Springs for a vacation.

October 6, 1924. Katheryne McClellan was named Macon County chair of Tennessee Democratic Women.

October 23, 1924. Former Tennessee Governor Ben W. Cooper attended a Republican barbecue at Red Boiling Springs where he was guest of honor. A large crowd of Republicans came from across the area and took part in the event.

October 27, 1924. Democrats were speaking across the state promoting their candidates in the final days of the 1924 election cycle. Former State Legislators John Grady Jones of Waverly and Robert Garland Draper of Gainesboro spoke at Red Boiling Springs.

August 26, 1925. Davidson County Judge Litton Hickman returned to his Nashville home after taking a few days rest in Red Boiling Springs. Hickman also chaired the State Fair Board of Commissioners.

September 3, 1925. United States Representative Robert Young Thomas from Kentucky, age 70, died at Red Boiling Springs. Thomas had served in Washington since 1916. He had been stricken with a "liver and kidney attack" and was brought to Red Boiling Springs on August 28. His condition grew steadily worse and he died during the late afternoon of September 3.

July 25, 1928. F. E. St. John, a Cullman, Alabama attorney, stopped in Nashville after his vacation in Nashville. St. John told Nashville reporters that while at the resort he had met people from all over Tennessee and they were all for Governor Henry Horton's reelection. Either St. John was overstating the situation or those supporting the Governor's opponents all vacationed elsewhere. Horton won reelection, but his vote total was unimpressive. In Macon County, Horton only received about half as many votes as his Republican opponent, Raliegh S. Hopkins.

September 17, 1928. Raliegh S. Hopkins, the GOP nominee for Governor, spoke at Red Boiling Springs. Hopkins carried Macon County, but had no real chance of overcoming the huge Democratic majority in the Volunteer State.

August 13, 1929. Montgomery County, Tennessee County Judge John T. Cummingham, and the superintendent of Montgomery County rural schools, A. W. Jobe, were taking an extended vacation at Red Boiling Springs.

August 28, 1931. US Senator and future US Secretary of State, Cordell Hull and war hero Alvin C. York attended the Austin Peay Memorial Highway Association at Red Boiling Springs.

June 26, 1932. Candidate for the Democratic nomination for Governor, Lewis S. Pope, spoke to more than 1,000 people at Red Boiling Springs. He was in a tight contest with Tennessee State Treasurer Hill McAlister and he expressed confidence that he would win. The primary was close, but McAlister defeated Pope by about 10,000 votes. Another candidate, former Governor,

Malcomb Patterson may have drawn enough votes to ensure McAlister's nomination. Pope then ran in the November contest as an independent. McAlister was elected and Pope finished a distant third.

August 30, 1932. Chairman of the Davidson County Board of Education, S. P. Johnson, was vacationing at Red Boiling Springs.

September 5, 1932. Congressman John Ridley Mitchell spoke in favor of enacting federal legislature to benefit veterans during an address at Red Boiling Springs.

September 15, 1935. Speaker of the United States House of Representatives, Joseph W. "Jo" Byrns and his spouse Julia arrived at Red Boiling Springs for a weekend of relaxation.

July 4, 1936. Speaker of the US House of Representatives Joseph W. "Jo" Byrnes died suddenly on June 4, 1936. Naturally, since it was an election year, there was a scramble among those wishing take the seat in the November. Former District Attorney General Richard Merrill Atkinson was the first candidate for the seat to go on a speaking tour. Atkinson, a candidate for the Democratic nomination spoke at Red Boiling Springs at 8 p.m.

Atkinson won a competitive primary and then won the General Election virtually unopposed. However, he only served one term. In 1938, he lost in the Democratic primary to Jo Byrns, Jr.

July 9, 1936. Another Democratic candidate for the seat opened by the death of Jo Byrnes was Will T. Cheek. Cheek, a successful commodities dealer, named his county campaign managers. Cheek chose A. W. Richardson of Red Boiling Springs to manage his campaign in Macon County

October 25, 1937. State Representative D. M. Coleman of Chattanooga and Tennessee Governor Gordon Browning were both Democrats, but they were often at odds on important issues. It was good news for the Governor then when he learned that

Coleman wouldn't take any further part in the legislature's special session then in progress.

Coleman suffered from high blood pressure and was "quite nervous" and his doctor advised him to take a "complete rest." Coleman took his doctor's advice and went to Red Boiling Springs to recuperate.

June 22, 1938. It was an election year and many candidates were on the campaign trail. Governor Gordon Browning gave a midmorning speech at Red Boiling Springs.

June 28, 1938. Candidate for the Democratic nomination for Governor, Roy C. Wallace, spoke at Red Boiling Springs. In the Democratic Primary Prentice Cooper easily defeated Governor Browning, Wallace, and another candidate. Then, Cooper defeated Republican Howard Baker, Sr. by landslide proportions in the General Election. In fact, support for Cooper was so expansive that he carried the usually Republican voting Macon County.

July 5, 1938. Congressman Richard M. Atkinson began his uphill fight for reelection. That morning, he gave a speech at Red Boiling Springs.

July 26, 1938. Congressman J. Ridley Mitchell was seeking a seat in the US Senate. In a speech in Red Boiling Springs, Mitchell, a supporter of the policies of President Roosevelt, confidently predicted victory in the crowded Democratic primary.

Senator Nathan L. Bachman had died in office on April 23, 1937, and Governor Browning had appointed George L. Berry to the seat. Berry, the President of the International Printing Pressmen and Assistants' Union of North America, was seen as vulnerable and five others entered the Democratic Primary. Tom Stewart won the primary and then won the November General Election in a landslide.

July 27, 1938. "Jo" Byrns, Jr. was destined to hold the seat once occupied by his father. But first, he had to dispose of Richard M. Atkinson. To that end, Byrns gave an afternoon speech at Red Boiling Springs. Byrns defeated Atkinson in the Democratic primary and was then victorious in the November election.

July 7, 1940. District Attorney General J. Carlton Loser and spouse returned to their Nashville home after spending a happy Independence Day at Red Boiling Springs. In later years, Loser served in the United States House of Representatives.

July 24, 1940. Judge David L. Rosenau of Limestone County, Alabama was on vacation at Red Boiling Springs.

July 29, 1940. W. D. (Pete) Hudson was an experienced politician. He had won his seat on the Tennessee Railroad and Public Utilities Commission in a statewide election. In 1940, Hudson was trying to unseat 5th District Congressman "Jo" Byrns, Jr. in the Democratic primary. One of Hudson's campaign stops was at Red Boiling Springs. Despite Hudson's best efforts, Byrns won the primary.

October 23, 1940. J. Percy Priest spoke at Red Boiling Springs. Priest was a politically connected reporter working for a Nashville newspaper. Although Priest was a Democrat, he decided to run an independent campaign against Congressman "Jo" Byrnes, Jr. Priest selected Aubrey West to manage his campaign in Macon County where the candidate's independent status helped him. Priest surprised the pundits when he defeated Byrns in the General Election.

July 8, 1942. Former US Representative John Ridley Mitchell spoke at Red Boiling Springs. Mitchell had decided to try to unseat Governor Prentice Cooper in the Democratic primary. Mitchell hired Austin Peay, Jr. (the son of the former Governor) to manage his campaign and then he embarked on a whirlwind tour of Tennessee. Mitchell ran a surprisingly strong campaign, but Governor Cooper prevailed in the primary and then romped to reelection.

9. Business Affairs

Most Red Boiling Springs residents were farmers, but there were several businesses in the town besides the hotels. This chapter takes a brief look at some of those business enterprises.

April 16, 1902. Even though the hotels at Red Boiling Springs employed several people, they couldn't hire everyone that worked in the service industry. J. D. Smith of Red Boiling Springs was seeking employment as a bartender. His qualifications were that he was 50, he had two years of experience, he didn't drink, he had good references, and he was willing to relocate. Evidently, Smith quickly found employment slinging suds.

April 14, 1905. There was more going on in Red Boiling Springs than mere frivolity. People in Red Boiling Springs worked hard, and some of them sought ways to work better. J. M. Sutton was one of them. Although Red Boiling Springs wasn't exactly in cotton country, there was a small amount of it grown in Macon County. Sutton wanted to profit from the cotton business and he applied for and received a patent for a cotton chopper.

April 18, 1905. Macon County, Tennessee was gaining attention for its recent improvements. Farmers were "building better and more modern houses, barns and fences," and property values had increased at least 500%. There were several lumber companies doing exceptional business. One of them shipped about four million feet of hardwood lumber annually. There were several modern sawmills and a handle factory. Waterworks supplied water to the businesses on the Lafayette town square as well as to several private residences.

Lafayette College (prep school) was founded in 1901 and by 1905 it could accommodate 500 students. The county boasted a new courthouse (finished in 1901) and was building a new jail. The Macon County Fair was among the best in the state. Added to this, despite the growth and improvements, the Macon County government was sound and frugal. The county had a surplus of about $1,500 (more than $50,000 in today's dollars).

April 19, 1908. There are many artistic people in this world. Newspaper editor Bedford C. Hix of Red Boiling Springs was one of them. Hix also wanted to make money from his talents. He ran the following newspaper advertisement: "Your name in rainbow colors, on two multicolored, flower postcards, with complete instructions for doing such beautiful work for 10 cents."

April 2, 1909. The Union Telephone Company of Macon County "connected" with the Cumberland Telephone and Telegraph Company. The Cumberland discontinued its toll stations at Lafayette and Red Boiling Springs and ran their lines to both places into the Union Company switchboard. The merger was expected to improve service and lower costs for telephone users.

October 2, 1910. Several businesses in Red Boiling Springs were doing very well. McClure & Son had just received a complete boiler, engine, and sawmill outfit from John P. Dale Machinery Company in Nashville.

November 12, 1911. John P. Dale Machinery Company did good business with sawmills in Red Boiling Springs. The Dale company sent another "fine woodworking outfit" to a Red Boiling Springs milling concern.

February 9, 1913. George B. Graves diversified his business. His company, Graves and Pate owned one of the largest tracts of lumber in Tennessee. The tract was near Red Boiling Springs. During 1912, Graves entered the real estate business in Nashville. He had overseen the "building and selling of a number of houses" there. In his latest move, Graves purchased an interest and acted as a "working partner" in the Kennedy Brothers real estate firm.

February 13, 1913. Although no major waterway ambled through Macon County, much of the lumber and other goods leaving Red Boiling Springs went via the Cumberland River. Sawmills and other businesses hauled their goods by wagon the 15 to 20 miles to the landing at West Point, in Smith County. From there, the goods were floated down the river to Nashville. The river option wasn't ideal for businesses, but it was better than taking several days per trip by horsedrawn wagons.

March 2, 1913. The Hartsfeld Auto Company in Nashville had just completed a terrific week. Its agents had sold five Fords. One of the new Fords went to a driver in Red Boiling Springs.

October 2, 1913. The Red Boiling Springs Reality Company was incorporated. The company had a capital investment of $10,000 and the incorporators were J. B. Birdwell, C. C. Shoulders, H. L. Sandler, John Shoulders, "Bug" Shoulders, S. B. Crabtree, B. M. Crabtree, and J. Gains. Eventually, the company came to own the Red Boiling Springs Water Company and the Palace Hotel.

January 11, 1914. J. F. Allen of Red Boiling Springs, who had been a travelling salesman for the J. H. Orr Company, started his new job as traveling salesman for J. S. Reeves & Company. He sold wholesale dry goods, notions, and furnishings.

September 5, 1915. Tanlac was a patent medicine touted by the Cooper Medicine Company as being able to cure almost any malady. The company sold almost one million bottles of the cur-all in its first year. Cooper Medicine only offered one agency (franchise) per community, promising that the agent would never have any competition. Naturally, Red Boiling Springs offered a large potential market for Tanlac and the McClellan Brothers snapped up the franchise.

November 28, 1915. The Cumberland Motor Company in Nashville was one of the largest Dodge dealers in America. Not only did it sell cars in Nashville, but it had 17 associate dealerships spread across Middle Tennessee. The associate dealer in Red Boiling Springs was Charles Bancroft McClellan.

Producing some 45,000 vehicles, in 1915, Dodge was the third largest auto manufacturer in America. It trailed only Ford's automobile production of 501,492 and Willis-Overland's production of 91,904.

April 5, 1917. The Hix Realty Company of Nashville stated that it would auction off the 300-acre "Rhodes Farm" about half a mile from Red Bowling Springs. The farm had much to offer. It had access to two public roads, and a "good house and barn." The property could be sliced up into tracks, but there were reasons to leave it intact.

The Rhodes Farm appeared to be an ideal place to build a successful commercial enterprise. The real estate company spokesman stated that "Red Boiling Springs is Tennessee's leading health resort and is rapidly and surely growing into a city. It has built more houses in the last two years than any other town of twice its size in the state. It has good schools, churches, splendid stores, mills and factories, electric lights and other modern conveniences."

The property itself possessed "fine freestone springs, and as fine sulphur water as can be found in the town" of Red Boiling Springs. The belief was that it was "a good location for a great sanatorium – an institution with unlimited possibility at Red Boiling Springs." It was also "an ideal place for a great hotel. The four big hotels already here cannot accommodate" all the vacationers coming to Red Boiling Springs.

March 22, 1919. The Red Boiling Springs Bank was incorporated with capital stock of $12,500 (about a quarter of a million dollars in today's currency). On April 3, the following bank officers were named: B. M. Chitwood, President; H.C. Hesson, Vice President; Avery Clark, cashier; and S. B. Crabtree, Charles Bancroft McClellan, R. P. Clark, H. L. Sandler, A. P. Parkhurst, R. R. Clark, B. C. Trousdale, and J. B. Braswell, Directors.

November 30, 1919. Pathé was one of the world's leading phonograph producers. The McClellan Brothers were the Pathé dealers in Red Boiling Springs. The enterprising brothers were also Macon County's authorized Ford dealers.

Besides their business dealings in Red Boiling Springs, the McClellan Brothers were spending $10,000 (more than $180,000 in today's currency) to build a brick garage on a corner lot of the Lafayette Public Square. Red Boiling Springs merchant Otis Parkhurst would "have charge" of the garage.

June 23, 1921. The I. J. Cooper Rubber Company was a major distributor of automotive batteries. Cooper batteries were sold in Red Boiling Springs at the service station owned by Charles C. Chitwood and Company.

January 7, 1922. Otis Parkhurst had a "Wiley Light Plant" generator which he used to charge automobile batteries. He stated that the generator had more than paid for itself.

August 23, 1922. Sawmills have always been an important industry at Red Boiling Springs. The work is labor intensive and very dangerous. On the afternoon of August 23, Gene Knight, age 18, an employee of J. B. Bruck Company, was cutting a large slab with a ripsaw. The slab became bound up in the saw and then it shot out and struck the young man in the abdomen, rupturing his intestines. Sawmill personnel rushed Knight to the Protestant Hospital in Nashville where a surgeon performed an emergency operation.

November 7, 1922. The Model 866 Delco-Light Powerplant Generator was still selling at the 1920 price of $175 each. The Chitwood Brothers were the distributors of the generators in Red Boiling Springs.

December 1, 1922. Tennessee State Treasurer, Hill McAlister, reported that $1,010 of the state's General Fund was deposited in the Red Boiling Springs Bank and that the bank had paid the state $10 in interest.

By June 1, 1923, the amount of the General Fund in the Red Boiling Springs Bank had risen to $3,022.50 and the interest the bank had paid was $12.50.

On December 1, 1923, the amount of General fund money in the Red Boiling Springs Bank had fallen to $2,573.35 and $1.25 in interest had been paid.

July 22, 1923. E. A. Butt of Portland, Tennessee had a seven-room bungalow for rent in Red Boiling Springs. The bungalow was wired for electricity, and was centrally located. The property also had outbuildings. Butt was offering the property for $1,400 per year and would provide "good terms" for anyone that acted quickly.

November 23, 1923. Palmolive introduced a new product – an after shaving talc designed to keep the skin smooth and remove the "after shave shine." The company promoted the product by selling it with other products at a discount. The package included 10¢ soap, 35¢ shaving cream, and the 25¢ talc. The company sold the collection valued at 70¢ for 49¢.

The Chitwood Brothers sold the new shaving talc in Red Boiling Springs.

January 18, 1924. Business was booming in Red Boiling Springs and most commercial enterprises there expected record years. Hudson & Chitwood had opened a new establishment. Charles B. McClellan reported that 1923 was his best year ever. The Chitwood Brothers had remodeled their store and their sales were brisk. R. R. Clark sold his property to Ellis Witcher and had moved to Gallatin and opened a new grocery store.

February 4, 1924. Powell & Davis planned to open a new grocery store in Red Boiling Springs. They stated that they would build the store as soon as the weather permitted and would stock it soon thereafter.

Cancel Deckard was also building a new store building. By early March, the building was almost completed and Deckard said he'd be stocking it soon.

February 7, 1924. Preparations were underway to increase both tobacco and cotton production throughout Macon County, including Red Boiling Springs. The prospect of increased cotton production caused quite a stir among local farmers and many who had never cultivated it before set aside land for use as cotton fields. Area banks backed the idea of increasing crop production, especially the production of cotton and several loans were made to farmers for that purpose.

February 20, 1924. Johnny Whitley's store at Red Boiling Springs burned during the night. The monetary loss suffered was unknown. Whitley had "some" insurance on the merchandise, but the building belonged to Logan Sadler and it was uninsured.

February 27, 1924. Katheryne McClellan was in Nashville purchasing women's hats for the spring line to be sold at McCellan Brothers in Red Boiling Springs. On March 8, the store opened a department dedicated to selling "many pretty hats for the coming season." Katheryne McClellan ran the department.

York and West had purchased, inventoried, and taken possession of the merchandise belonging to S. A. Newberry.

March 6, 1924. Clark and Archer were adding a line of women's hats to their "already immense stock of merchandise."

In order to keep up with other stores in Red Boiling Springs, the Chitwood Brothers were adding several items to their already wide selection of merchandise.

March 8, 1924. At least 16 travelling salesmen were in Red Boiling Springs visiting with various merchants.

June 1, 1924. The portion of the Tennessee General Fund at the Red Boiling Springs was $5,116.23, and the interest received was $42.50.

July 14, 1924. The Smith County Electric Company began running a line to Red Boiling Springs to furnish power to electrify homes and businesses in the town. The plan was for the line to be finished quickly. The company met its deadline and select areas of Red Boiling Springs had power by October 11.

December 1, 1924. The part of the Tennessee General Fund in the Red Boiling Springs Bank was $4,191.25 and the interest paid was $75.

May 14, 1925. The Tennessee Bankers' Association was holding its annual convention in Nashville. W. G. Birdwell, cashier of the Red Boiling Springs Bank, attended the convention.

June 1, 1925. The part of the Tennessee General Fund in the Red Boiling Springs Bank was $3,630.24 and the interest paid was $38.99.

September 7, 1925. Cassetty Oil and Grease Company distributed Apex Motor Oil to garages across Middle Tennessee. The Russell Brothers garage was the exclusive Apex Oil dealers in Red Boiling Springs. On September 13, John Lowe, President of Cassetty Oil and Grease was "spending a few days at Red Boiling Springs while the price of gasoline is getting located."

February 11, 1926. Will Burbage of Carthage was named manager of the Carthage Division of the Tennessee Electric Power Company. Red Boiling Springs was served by Burbage's division.

April 11, 1926. Even though Red Boiling Springs was world famous for its mineral waters, there was still a market for patent medicines there. One very popular patent medicine was called Dr. Anderson's Herb Tonic. It was claimed that the herb tonic would build up people recovering from the flu and most other ailments.

The Chitwood Brothers were the exclusive distributor of Dr. Anderson's Herb Tonic in Red Boiling Springs.

May 2, 1927. While telephones had been around for decades, shopping by telephone was a new and revolutionary idea. Lebeck Brothers Dry Goods in Nashville was having a big sale in celebration of its fifty-third anniversary. Store owners felt they could increase sales greatly if they could reach more out of town customers and the telephone seemed an ideal way to do it. The store offered nice discounts to any customer that placed an order via telephone.

But there was more. Lebeck Brothers cut a deal with Southern Bell Telephone & Telegraph to provide residents of southern Kentucky, middle Tennessee, and northern Alabama with reduced rates if they called the store long distance, station-to-station. The cost for Red Boiling Springs residents to call the store was 55¢.

September 29, 1927. The Red Boiling Springs Bank was to have a new home. It was going to move across the street into a new brick building more suitable for a business of its stature.

October 24, 1927. Macon County held a "livestock week." The perception was that the number of livestock (cattle, swine, sheep, etc.) in Macon County was far below what it should be. Teacher of vocational agriculture and local entrepreneur, W. E. Hix, led the push to increase the number of livestock in Macon County. During livestock week there were meetings across the county. The meeting in Red Boiling Springs took place on October 28 and more than 100 people attended.

Some of the speakers during livestock week were Homer Hancock, State Commissioner of Agriculture; J. R. McLeod of the University of Tennessee Agricultural Extension Office; C. C. Flannery, sheep specialist; Professor D. M. Clements, leader of the Tennessee Department of Agriculture; and Joel B. Ford, Managing Director of the Nashville Branch of the Federal Reserve Bank.

February 12, 1928. More commercial construction was underway in Red Boiling Springs. Cascar McLerran was building a new bakery in in town.

May 31, 1928. Henry Ford personally chose Veedol Motor Oil to be the official oil for all Ford vehicles. Since there were more Fords on the highway than any other automobile, Veedol "economy" oil was very popular. Fred Russell sold Veedol Motor Oil in Red Boiling Springs.

September 9, 1928. While the resort business in Red Boiling Springs provided many jobs for locals, it could not provide employment to everyone that wanted it. A man identifying himself as "Charlie" was looking for work as either a chauffeur or a houseman. Charlie, who got his mail at Cloyd Place, made a point of telling prospective employers that he was a white man.

December 1, 1928. The part of the Tennessee General Fund in the Red Boiling Springs Bank was $3,086.87 and the interest paid was $38.

January 2, 1929. The year got off to a bad start in Red Boiling Springs. A wicked fire destroyed or damaged several local businesses. The building housing the Knight Brothers bus station, B. P. Smith's restaurant, and Smith Brothers Hardware was destroyed. Additionally, Newt Knight's residence which was adjacent to the building was also burned beyond repair. Besides losing their bus terminal, the Knight Brothers lost three trucks and two buses.

Before a hastily formed bucket brigade manned by local volunteers brought the fire under control, Chitwood Brothers Hardware was destroyed and other businesses greatly damaged included the Gallatin Milling Company, and York's billiard parlor and barbershop.

April 22, 1929. The third annual banquet of the Tennessee Hotel Men was held at Nashville's beautiful Hermitage Hotel.

Association President Frank Schutt appointed a committee to nominate new officers for the coming year. The committee members were Frank Davis, manager of Nashville's Sam Davis Hotel, M. W. Thorton of Fayetteville, and Henry Counts of the Palace Hotel at Red Boiling Springs.

The conference of hotel proprietors continued through April 23.

June 20, 1929. There was a furnished "camp bungalow" for rent at Red Boiling Springs. It could be leased monthly, weekly, or the entire season.

July 24, 1929. The Hudson Motor Car Company produced a big six-cylinder car called the Essex Challenger. The Challenger was roomy, comfortable, featured handsome upholstery, and fine appointments, and came in a variety of colors. Other standard features included hydraulic shocks, 4-wheel brakes, radiator shutters, an air filter, a "glare proof" rear view mirror, safety lock, electric starter, fuel and oil gauge on the dash, and chrome plated parts. The manufacturer estimated the savings on the extra features to be $100.

The Essex was also speedy and powerful for its time. It had a top speed of 70 m.p.h. and could cruise at 60 m.p.h. "all day long." It could also climb steep hills with ease.

The factory price of the Essex was $695 and up, which was more than many people could afford. A basic Ford Model-A in 1929 went for about $385. Expensive or not, the Chitwood Brothers in Red Boiling Springs offered the Essex Challenger for sale.

September 20, 1929. The Tennessee Railroad and Public Utilities Commission approved a request by the Tennessee Electric Power Company to reduce its rates by 10 to 30 percent. More than 100 Middle Tennessee towns, including Red Boiling Springs, benefitted from the rate cut.

September 21, 1929. The founders of the Jacksonian Hotel Company incorporated it with a capital investment of $60,000 (almost $1.1 million in today's currency). They also chose officers and a board of directors. Henry Counts of the Palace Hotel was one of those elected to the board.

April 13, 1930. The Chitwood Brothers were the Red Boiling Springs distributor of the Hudson Great 8 automobile. Hudson Motor Company claimed the car was the most economical 8-cylinder vehicle on the market. The car was noted for its quick takeoff and the ease with which it could maneuver in hilly terrain. The vehicle could achieve speeds of up to 80 m.p.h., had a wheelbase of between 119 and 126 inches, could get between 15 and 18 miles per gallon, and a set of tires would last for up to 20,000 miles.

Standard equipment included four two-way shock absorbers, radiator shutters, a starter on the dash, an "electrolock," electric fuel and oil gauges on the dash, a tire lock, and a luggage rack. As with other automobiles built at the Hudson factory in Detroit, the Great 8 came in a variety of colors. Depending upon which of the ten versions a customer wanted, the Great 8 carried a sticker price of between $1,050 and $1,650 factory direct.

Chitwood Brothers continued to offer the Essex Challenger as well, but the price had increased from the previous year. Its price ranged from $735 to $995. Those wanting a model with a "commercial chassis" could have it for an additional $445. Hudson claimed the Challenger was a great bargain because it was as good as any $3,000 car.

By the end of August of 1930, the Hudson Motor Company had rethought its prices. The company reduced the base price of its Great 8 from $1,050 to $885 and it cut the base price of the Essex Challenger to $650.

October 30, 1930. The chancery court named M. D. Jones receiver of the bankrupt Nashville Tom Thumb Golf Company, Inc. The Liberty Bank & Trust Company had initiated the action. The bank asserted that the golf company owed it about $5,000 and had as much as $2,000 in other debts. According to the bank, Tom Thumb's principal assets amounted to only about $2,000 in the form of two miniature golf courses. One was at Twenty-first Avenue South in Nashville and the other was in Red Boiling Springs at the Palace Hotel.

December 1, 1930. The part of the Tennessee General Fund in the Red Boiling Springs Bank was down to $1,112.46 and the interest paid was $46.50.

May 26, 1931. The Nashville Booster Club began its twenty-first annual tour of Middle Tennessee towns with the stated purpose of promoting business interests in the region. The boosters arrived at Red Boiling Springs at 6:30 p.m. and left on the morning of May 27 at 8 o'clock.

April 24, 1932. The Leonard electric refrigerator company offered the public an innovation. It featured what it called a "Len-a-Door." A housewife, even with her hands full, could open her refrigerator with just "a touch of her toe." Leonard offered full-sized models as well as nine portable models. Fred's Garage, operated by Fred Russell, was the Leonard dealer in Red Boiling Springs.

Naturally, Fred's Garage didn't specialize in refrigerators. Its main line included Gulf gasoline, motor oil, Firestone tires and innertubes, and automotive accessories. The garage, located at the entrance to Red Boiling Springs, featured an "expert mechanical department" and a 24-hour wrecker service. The garage staff also washed and polished cars for waiting motorists.

July 24, 1932. S. A. Chitwood & Sons Drugs and Soda was thriving in Red Boiling Springs.

February 11, 1933. Governor McAlister appointed committees in all Tennessee counties to provide Reconstruction Finance Corporation relief loans. W. A. Jordan of Red Boiling Springs was named to the Macon County committee.

July 9, 1933. Fred's Garage continued to offer all types of service to those motoring to Red Boiling Springs.

July 26, 1934. F. B. Lacey, Field Representative of the Agricultural Adjustment Act tobacco control division, spoke at Red Boiling Springs. Lacey was attempting to get more people to take part in the Agricultural Adjustment Act tobacco acreage signup. Macon County was lagging behind in the signup and Lacey was striving to get as many aboard with the program as possible before the July 28 deadline.

October 28, 1935. A. W. Richardson of Red Boiling Springs sold building materials including two by fours, two by sixes, and two by eights to Nashvillians for $1.90 per hundred and up. Richardson delivered the materials to Nashville personally and his business was quite successful.

February 18, 1936. The estate of Henry Counts was in dispute. The People's Bank of Scottsville, Kentucky claimed the Counts estate owed it $10,940 with 6% annual interest to be added from January 31, 1931, or $15,518.60 total (more than $300,000 in today's currency). Henry's widow, Eva Counts, who was the administrator of the estate, along with R. W. Comer and G. L. Comer, both of Nashville, and Dr. L. O. Johnson, Ed F. Welch, and W. D. Fowler all of Scottsville, Kentucky filed a lawsuit in the District Court at Scottsville to prevent the bank from collecting the debt.

June 1, 1937. The part of the Tennessee General Fund in the Red Boiling Springs Bank was $5,027.32 and the interest paid was $50.02.

November 9, 1937. The Warren County, Kentucky and Bowling Green Burley Boosters were making a tour to promote increased tobacco production. Although their primary concern was production in Kentucky, the group visited several Tennessee towns as well – including Red Boiling Springs.

June 1, 1938. The part of the Tennessee General Fund in the Red Boiling Springs Bank was $5,000 with no interest paid.

June 7, 1938. The Tennessee Railroad and Public Utilities Commission approved a contract between the Tennessee Electric Power Company and the Tri-County Electric Membership Cooperative for power at Red Boiling Springs. The cost to build a power substation and new power lines would be $21,500. In all, Tri-County intended to string 245 miles of power lines in Clay, Macon, Sumner, and Trousdale counties. Construction began on July 1.

August 6, 1938. Bruce Wood of Red Boiling Springs was trying to sell what he claimed was a genuine Stradivarius violin. Today, there are only 450-512 genuine Stradivarius violins still in existence and they are worth millions of dollars each.

September 29, 1938. The Philco Radio Company promoted what it called its "Mystery Control." The Mystery Control was a battery powered wireless remote control that with a touch of a fingertip could change up to eight stations on a Philco radio. Beyond that, it could adjust the volume and turn the radio off from several feet away – even from another room. Today, remotes are no big deal, but in 1938, the Mystery Control was billed as "sensational. thrilling, breathtaking."

Dewey Slate was the Philco dealer in Red Boiling Springs.

November 6, 1938. The Tennessee Naturopathic Association chose its officers for the coming year. Dr. Royal A. Leslie of Red Boiling Springs was elected Vice President of the organization.

Naturopaths are educated in the basic sciences and offer complementary and alternative treatments, focusing on "body, mind and spirit." Naturopaths also focus on "the body's natural ability to heal itself." Traditional naturopathy avoided drugs and surgery. While naturopathic doctors in past times were helpful to patients, especially in those communities with few MDs, their training was far below that offered by medical schools.

June 1, 1939. The portion of the Tennessee General Fund held at the Red Boiling Springs Bank was $5,000.

January 27, 1940. The Red Boiling Springs Bank won a judgment in Chancery Court against the Tennessee Acceptance Corporation.

June 1, 1940. The portion of the Tennessee General Fund held at the Red Boiling Springs Bank was still $5,000.

July 4, 1941. The Tennessee Rural Letter Carriers Association ended their annual convention that was held that year at Nashville's Andrew Jackson Hotel. J. W. Bean of ed Boiling Springs was elected President of the group for the next term.

December 6, 1941. W. A. Jordan of Red Boiling Springs offered "genuine hickory smoked country hams" for sale for 35¢ per pound. Jordan had hams of several sizes

December 1, 1943. The portion of the Tennessee General Fund held at the Red Boiling Springs Bank remained $5,000.

December 31, 1943. The Airlines of Tennessee, Inc. received a charter to do business in the Volunteer State. The initial capital investment was only $1,000, but the company intended to issue 2,000 shares of stock without nominal or par value. The stock offering was intended to raise enough money to purchase the equipment necessary to operate the air service. Dr. Royal A. Leslie of Red Boiling Springs was one of the incorporators of the airline.

May 8, 1945. "Spred" wall paint, manufactured by the Glidden paint company, was billed as "extra durable and washable." One coat, it was claimed, would cover most surfaces, including wallpaper, and one gallon would paint a room of 10 feet by 14 feet. The paint, which came in 11 colors, was sold in Red Boiling Springs at Chitwood Hardware and Drug Store.

CL Gammon

10. Weather, War and Other Things

This chapter looks at some things of interest, such as weather events, not covered in the other chapters that happened at Red Boiling Springs between 1900 and 1945. There were several residents of Red Boiling Springs killed and wounded in the World Wars who are not included here. You can find a listing of the World War II dead and wounded CL Gammon's book *Highland Rim Warriors: Macon County, Tennessee, and World War II.*

November 23, 1906. Macon County Trustee, Larkin Nathan Smith died. Only 32, Smith had assumed his duties only a couple of months before. He was also married in 1906. He was buried in the Smith Chapel Cemetery at Red Boiling Springs.

June 5, 1907. At about 11:50 a.m. Southern Railway train Number 16 from Nashville derailed about three and one-half miles from Lebanon. It was the first crash involving a Southern Railway train near Nashville since the company took over the Tennessee Central line.

None of the crew or 54 passengers were killed, but 20 were hurt. Five passengers were seriously injured. Those that suffered the worst injuries were rushed to Nashville and admitted to St. Thomas Hospital. The passengers that were not in need of emergency care were taken to Nashville's Tulane Hotel. Mattie Beasley of Red Boiling Springs was among those taken to the hotel.

September 29, 1909. John H. Dale of Clay County, Tennessee spent a week at the Tennessee State Fair and on his way home he dropped in on his brother A. C. Dale at Red Boiling Springs. During the visit, John, who had appeared to be in fine health, died suddenly.

February 23, 1922. Charles C. Davis took and passed the Civil Service exam. Afterward, US Representative Wynne F. Clouse recommended that Davis be named postmaster at Red Boiling Springs.

July 30, 1925. The Women's Bible Study Class of Red Boiling Springs held a memorial service for William Jennings Bryan. Bryan had agreed to speak at the Teachers' Institute at Epperson Springs on July 26, but had cancelled because of a conflict in his schedule. Ironically, he happened to die on the day he was scheduled to speak there.

September 7, 1926. Tennessee State Archaeologist, P. E. Cox was attempting to develop evidence that prehistoric men lived in North America at least as early as they lived in Europe. To prove his hypothesis Cox led expeditions to Leonard Cave and Taylor's Cave near Red Boiling Springs where he found evidence that prehistoric people used the large cavern as both a dwelling place and a burial ground.

Critics scoffed at Cox. Some said that he claimed the area around Red Boiling Springs was the location of the Garden of Eden. Cox never made any such assertion.

The dig eventually located the skeletons of adults, one of which Cox called "one of the most ancient ever found in America, of a distinctly brute type." He also found flint implements as well as fossils and "petrified" turtles. Cox's findings were important because they proved that Native Americans were in the area near Red Boiling Springs thousands of years before the first European settler came to North America. However the evidence indicated that humans came to North America long after the Neanderthals appeared in Europe.

September 15, 1926. There was a large rally for Tennessee's Republican gubernatorial nominee Walter White in Cookeville. Republican dignitaries, including former Governors from both Tennessee and Kentucky spoke in White's behalf. Red Boiling Springs did its part in the effort. It sent a big brass band to entertain the audience. White carried Macon County narrowly, but Democratic Governor, Austin Peay won the election statewide with ease.

December 21, 1926. In what was considered Tennessee's worst continuous downpour in more than a decade, two days of rain flooded large portions of the state. Many acres of farmland was under water and many roads were impassable.

In Red Boiling Springs, Salt Lick Creek roared from its banks and threatened homes and businesses. Angry torrents of water virtually isolated the town. The main street was blocked and Christmas shopping was put off until later. More importantly, the raging stream blocked the approach to the bridge leading into town causing the cancellation of bus service from Nashville and preventing mail deliveries. Several residents were forced from their homes, but there were no serious injuries reported.

The flood also inundated the electric power company in Carthage causing power outages in Red Boiling Springs.

March 18, 1927. The area around Red Boiling Springs was faced with a rabies epidemic. Believed to have been introduced by foxes and other wild animals, hydrophobia first appeared in dogs. The mad dogs bit livestock infecting many of them as well. Worse than that, at 17 people had to take the painful regimen of shots to prevent rabies. The Pasteur Treatment was an ordeal, but without it, those infected with rabies were virtually certain to die.

Rabies remained a problem in and around Red Boiling Springs for decades.

July 2, 1928. Tennessee State Treasurer Hill McAlister, a candidate for the Democratic nomination for Governor, took his campaign to Gainesboro and spoke there. Although it was thought to be a stronghold of Governor Horton, some 344 people turned out to greet McAlister. A brass band from Red Boiling Springs entertained the crowd.

Horton supporters lambasted McAlister because he had some Republicans in his camp. Two of those Republicans were S. A. and

B. W. Chitwood. The two accompanied McAlister on his Upper Cumberland tour to Cookeville. One Horton operative said, "B. W. Chitwood is the owner of the Donoho Hotel at Red Boiling Springs and it is one of the best resort hotels in the state, but he is a Republican." S. A. Chitwood was a candidate for the Republican State Committee from the Fourth Congressional District.

Governor Horton, who also courted Republican voters, defeated McAllister in a narrow primary contest.

March 17, 1929. A man identified as "Lieutenant Warner" was planning to drive from Red Boiling Springs to California. Warner was looking for a "gentleman" to make the trip with him. He insisted that those wishing to accompany him provide references. The journey would begin on March 21.

March 26, 1929. There was another round of flooding at Red Boiling Springs. Although the flooding in the resort town was not as great as it was in some nearby communities, it was worse than the flood of 1926. Roads were blocked by torrents of water and telephone service was interrupted.

April 23, 1931. Former editor of the *Macon County News*, Bedford C. Hix died at the Veterans' Hospital in Alexanderia, Louisiana. He was about 42 and he suffered from what was described as "tuberculosis of the throat." Before the age of 25, Hix built the circulation of his paper to more than 2,000. He was also active in community affairs. As noted earlier, Hix was at the forefront of improving the road from Lafayette to Red Boiling Springs.

Mystery still surrounds Hix. Sometime about 1921, Hix, who was never married, abandoned his home and business and no one heard from him until a few days before his death. The mystery of why he suddenly forsook his life in Macon County remains unsolved.

April 25, 1932. Colonel Henry Dickinson toured several Upper Cumberland communities attempting to stir interest in a mass meeting to be held in Nashville. The purpose of the rally was to push for federal legislation granting bonuses to World War I veterans. Red Boiling Springs was one of the towns Dickinson visited.

May 9, 1933. A terrible tornado struck Tompkinsville, Kentucky killing eight and leaving more than a score of others injured. It was feared that the tornado had ravished Red Boiling Springs as well, but no one knew for several hours because telephone communications between Red Boiling Springs and the outside world were knocked out. Thankfully, Red Boiling Springs was largely spared damage.

March 19, 1934. The worst ice storm in memory struck Middle Tennessee. A sheet of ice covered Red Boiling Springs. Power and telephone service was knocked out across the town and traffic was slowed because of slippery roads and downed trees.

June 14, 1936. Most of Tennessee had been without rain for more than two months. Farmers in The Volunteer State had already lost about one-quarter of their crops with an estimated value of between forty and fifty million dollars ($850 million to $1.1 billion in today's currency).

Desperate times require desperate acts and Elder E. C. Butler of Red Boiling Springs decided that everyone appeal to God for relief. Citing the New Testament (James 5:17-18) Butler asked all Christians to pray for rain at exactly 11 a.m.

September 8, 1936. Creed Clements, age 20, of Clay County received serious injuries in an automobile accident near Red Boiling Springs. He was riding in a pickup truck with Will King when it collided head on with a car driven by Dillard Maxey. Willie Hunter was a passenger in Maxey's car.

Clements was the only person serious injured in the accident. He suffered scalp wounds and a fractured skull. Instead of being taken to a hospital, Clements was transported to the Palace Hotel where he received treatment from the resident physician.

March 14, 1938. Chancery Court Judge A. F. Officer heard a case brought by Macon County against the Bank of Red Boiling Springs. Former Macon County Trustee Wash Patterson asserted that the bank had wrongly charged his office $1,000 in 1934 and the county was attempting to recover the money.

May 20, 1938. 2,100 soldiers of the Seventh Cavalry Brigade, the only mechanized military unit of its kind in the United States, departed its home base at Fort Knox, Kentucky and rolled to Cookeville, Tennessee. Residents of Red Boiling Springs lined the highway to watch the eight hour procession of combat cars, mortar mounts, field artillery pieces, howitzers, motorcycles, trucks, and personnel carriers pass by.

February 14, 1939. Representatives of the trucking industry went before a joint committee of the State House and Senate and offered to accept a tax increase in exchange for an increase in the maximum weight they could carry. They wanted an increase from 18,000 pounds to 36,000 pounds. S. W. Harris of Red Boiling Springs testified that the 18,000 pound limit made it impossible for him to haul lumber at a profit.

October 17, 1940. With America's first ever peacetime draft underway, every county in had a draft board. Red Boiling Springs doctor H. C. Hesson was the physician on the Macon County draft board.

September 18, 1941. The military proposed building an army base at Clarksville. The sticking point was providing the camp with the 5,000,000 gallons of water it would require daily. The most reasonable fix for the water problem was to pump it either from the Red River or from Red Boiling Springs. The camp is known as Fort Campbell today.

September 5, 1942. The United States Army was having full-scale training exercises in Middle Tennessee which were referred to as "maneuvers." The Army issued a warning that any motorist driving faster than 35 m.p.h. in the maneuver zone would be arrested. At times, all of Red Boiling Springs was in the maneuver zone.

January 3, 1943. Widespread flooding affected most of Middle Tennessee. While the flooding was worse in towns along the Cumberland River, other areas were impacted as well. Highway 56 between Gainesboro and Red Boiling Springs was closed due to high water. It remained impassable until January 8.

Conclusion to Part 2

I hope you have enjoyed this book about the wonderful Red Boiling Springs and maybe learned a little about this little town.

Part 3 will pick up the story in 1946, and it will continue to trace the evolution of this great little town. If you have read the first two parts of this story, you can easily see the growth of the community, in sophistication, if not in population. Part 3 will shine light on the continued growth of our grand, but tiny, Red Boiling Springs.

Selected Sources

"Actors on the Screen of Commerce." *The Nashville American*, September 13, 1925, p. 36.

"A Delightful Place to Spend September and October, *The Nashville Tennessean and The Nashville American*, September 11, 1916, p. 10.

"Addresses Voters of Macon County, *The Nashville American*, August 3, 1910, p. 2.

"Advertising Tennessee Resorts." *The Nashville American*, May 17, 1906, p. 10.

"Agents." *The Nashville Tennessean*, May 14, 1929, p. 7.

"Airplanes Will Lead the Drive to 'Fill Stadium.'" *The Nashville Tennessean*, October 8, 1925, p. 1.

"A July Christmas at Red Boiling Springs." *The Nashville Tennessean*, and *The Nashville American*, July 16, 1916, p. B-9.

Alexander, T. H. "By the Way." *The Nashville Tennessean*, August 1, 1922, p. 4.

Alexander, T. H. "By the Way." *The Nashville Tennessean*, August 6, 1922, p. 4.

Alexander, T. H. "By the Way." *The Nashville Tennessean*, July 1, 1922, p. 4.

Alexander, T. H. "By the Way." *The Nashville Tennessean*, July 30, 1925, p. 4.

Alexander, T. H. "I Reckon So." *The Nashville Tennessean*, August 19, 1929, p. 4.

Alexander, T. H. "Politics." *The Nashville Tennessean*, pp. 1, 5.

"All Political Races Speeded." *The Nashville Tennessean*, July 25, 1938, pp. 1-2.

"A Money Maker." *The Nashville Tennessean*, March 13, 1924, p. 15.

"A Most Delightful Trip." *The Nashville Tennessean and The Nashville American*, May 30, 1914, p. 7.

"Amusements are Planned for Red Boiling Springs." *The Nashville Tennessean*, March 14, 1924, p. 15.

"Amusements." *The Nashville Tennessean and The Nashville American*, May 21, 1915, p. 5.

"... and You Need Not be a Juggler." *The Nashville Tennessean*, April 24, 1932, p. 30.

"An Excellent Place to Recuperate from the Flu." *The Nashville Tennessean*, March 24, 1929, p. 73.

"Announcing Opening Dance." *The Nashville Tennessean*, May 16, 1926, p. 3.

"Another Railroad Company." *The Nashville American*, May 13, 1909, p. 8.

"Apex Motor Oil." *The Nashville American*, September 7, 1927, p. 7.

"Apostles of Good Roads are at Home Again." *The Nashville Tennessean*, and *The Nashville American*, August 4, 1913, p. 11.

"Appointments of Deputies." *The Nashville American*, August 26, 1908, p. 8.

"Approval." *The Nashville Tennessean*, June 8, 1938, p. 9.

"A Railway Line Will be Built." The Nashville Tennessean, May 13, 1909, p. 2.

"Archie Wilkes, Shot Monday by Morgan, Dies." *The Nashville Tennessean*, July 12, 1918, p. 6.

"Are After It." *The Nashville American*, December 14, 1908, p. 13.

"Arlington Hotel." *The Nashville Tennessean*, July 20, 1924, p. 7.

"Atkinson to Speak." *The Nashville Tennessean*, July 4, 1936, p. 1.

"At Morning Session." *The Nashville Tennessean and The Nashville American*, September 13, 1912, p. 3.

"At Red Boiling Springs." *The Nashville American*, July 30, 1905, p. 6.

"At Red Boiling Springs." *The Nashville American*, June 7, 1900, p. 3.

"Auction." *The Nashville Tennessean*, October 2, 1942, p. 51.

"Austin Peay Road Groups Meets Today." *The Nashville Tennessean*, August 28, 1931, p. 1.

"Auto Club Units to be Organized." *The Nashville Tennessean*, July 18, 1927, p. 2.

"Automobile Oil Tax Attacked." *The Nashville Tennessean*, and *The Nashville American*, July 21, 1916, p. 10.

"Autoists to Meet at Red Boiling." *The Nashville Tennessean*, and *The Nashville American*, July 23, 1913, p. 12-B.

"Automobile Licenses." *The Nashville Tennessean and The Nashville American*, June 24, 1915, p. 9-C.

"Automobile Licenses." *The Nashville Tennessean and The Nashville American*, September 12, 1914.

"Back to 1917 Prices." *The Nashville Tennessean*, November 7, 1922, p. 3.

"Bankers Registered Here for State Convention." *The Nashville Tennessean*, May 14, 1925, p. 8.

"Bank Officers Elected." *The Nashville Tennessean*, April 3, 1919, p. 7.

"Begins Campaigns." *The Nashville Tennessean*, July 5, 1938, p. 14.

"Best Road Designated to Red Boiling Springs." *The Nashville Tennessean*, August 2, 1925, p. 6.

"Better Auto Roads to Red Boiling Springs." *The Nashville Tennessean*, and *The Nashville American*, August 1, 1913, p. 3.

"Better Auto Roads to Red Boiling Springs." *The Nashville Tennessean*, and *The Nashville American*, July 21, 1913, p. 3.

"Better Be Safe Than Sorry." *The Nashville Tennessean and The Nashville American*, June 22, 1913, p. 7-A.

"Bisons to Meet Freed-Hardeman." *The Nashville Tennessean*, January 17, 1942, p. 7.

Black, Diane, complier. *Tennessee Senators*. Nashville: Tennessee State Library and Archives, 2010, p. 65.

Blankenship, Harold G. *History of Macon Country, Tennessee.* Tompkinsville, Kentucky: Monroe County Press, 1986, pp. 87-95, 97, 113-117, 153, 155-156, 163.

"Black is Victor Over Greenspan in Boxing Meet." *The Nashville Tennessean*, December 15, 1936, p. 15.

"Blue Grass Bus Line Capitalized at $25,000." *The Nashville Tennessean*, April 24, 1926, p. 2.

"Board in Macon Picks Teachers." *The Nashville Tennessean*, April 30, 1937, p. 3.

"Board Organizes." *The Nashville American*, September 2, 1904, p. 3.

"Booster Club Makes Annual Tour." *The Nashville Tennessean*, April 28, 1931, p. 1.

"Boosting Good Roads Meeting." *The Nashville Tennessean*, and *The Nashville American*, July 29, 1913, p. 3.

"Both Dissatisfied." *The Nashville American*, April 14, 1904, p. 10.

"Bowling Green, Kentucky." *The Nashville Tennessean*, November 4, 1925, p. 1.

"Branch Plants Consolidated." *The Nashville Tennessean*, June 12, 1925, p. 9.

"Brief News Notes of Nashville Town." *The Nashville American*, August 24, 1910, p. 10.

"Bug Shoulders." *The Nashville Tennessean and The Nashville American*, April 19, 1914, p. 3-E.

"Building Gains in Industrial Review." *The Nashville Tennessean*, February 12, 1928, p. 9.

"Building Trade Notes." *The Nashville American*, October 30, 1909, p. 9.

"Build Yourself Up for the Winter's Work September at Cloyd's Place Red Boiling Springs." *The Nashville Tennessean and The Nashville American*, September 13, 1916, p. 12.

Bullard, Loring. *Healing Waters: Missouri's Historic Mineral Springs and Spas.* Columbia, Missouri: University of Missouri Press, 2004, p. 96.

"Burbage Carthage Unit of Tennessee Power System." *The Nashville Tennessean*, February 12, 1926, p. 2.

"Burley Boosters Dip to Tennessee." *The Nashville Tennessean*, November 6, 1937, p. 2.

"Bus and Truck Line Permit Hearings are Set by Commission During April." *The Nashville Tennessean*, April 1, 1928, p. 67.

"Bus Excursion." *The Nashville Tennessean*, August 21, 1933, p. 5.

"Bus Line Permit is Given by Commission." *The Nashville Tennessean*, November 21, 1929, p. 7.

"Bus Line Petitions Heard by Utilities Commission." *The Nashville Tennessean*, September 12, 1931, p. 13.

"Bus Line Protests Unlicensed Firms." *The Nashville Tennessean*, October 17, 1929, p. 17.

"Bus Schedule." *The Nashville Tennessean*, May 30, 1926, p. 35.

"Byrnes Addresses Crowd Exhibit." *The Nashville Tennessean*, September 1935, p. 11.

"Cage Scores." *The Nashville Tennessean*, February 26, 1942, p. 13.

"Cage Scores, *The Nashville Tennessean*, January 16, 1942, p. 26.

"Cage Scores." *The Nashville Tennessean*, March 4, 1939, p. 6.

"Cage Scores." *The Nashville Tennessean*, March 3, 1939, p. 13.

"Camp Water Studied." *The Nashville Tennessean*, September 18, 1941, p. 18.

"Capt. C. A. Watkins, His Wife and Children Victims." *The Nashville Tennessean*, July 4, 1925, p. 4.

"Capt. John W. Morton Improving." *The Nashville American*, August 14, 1908, p. 10.

"Capt. John W. Morton." *The Nashville American*, July 3, 1908, p. 10.

"Capt. John Morton Returns." *The Nashville American*, August 18, 1908, p. 10.

"Carriers Elect." *The Nashville Tennessean*, April 22, 1932, p. 13.

"Carthage Support for Highway Plans Sought." *The Nashville Tennessean*, July 2, 1925, p. 3.

"Carthage." *The Nashville American*, May 16, 1909, p. 38.

"Carthage." *The Nashville American*, May 22, 1909, p. 9.

"C. B. McClellan, 51, Dies at Red Boiling Springs." *The Nashville Tennessean*, February 28, 1929, p. 2.

"Celebrate the 4th at the Palace Hotel." *The Nashville Tennessean*, July 4, 1934, p. 5.

"Celina Residents Abandon Homes." *The Nashville Tennessean*, March 26, 1929, p. 8.

"Central Hotel at Red Boiling Springs Sold." *The Nashville Tennessean*, May 25, 1918, p. 5.

Cervin, Michael. "Sulfur Springs: To Soak or Not to Soak." Fox News, October 28, 2015.

"Chamber Plans to Assume Work of Safety Body." *The Nashville Tennessean*, May 15, 1925, p. 1.

"Charters Issued." *The Nashville Tennessean*, and *The Nashville American*, October 2, 1913, p. 8.

"Charter to be Sought by Snipe Hunters." *The Nashville Tennessean and The Nashville American*, June 19, 1915, p. B-12.

"Chautauqua Begins Sunday at Red Boiling Springs." *The Nashville Tennessean,*

"Cheapest, Quickest and Most Pleasant Route to Red Boiling Springs." *The Nashville Tennessean and The Nashville American*, May 29, 1914, p. 8.

"Cheap Rates on the Excursion Steamer *Jo Horton Falls.*" *The Nashville Tennessean*, and *The Nashville American*, July 18, 1916, B-9.

"Cheek Names Managers." *The Nashville Tennessean*, July 10, 1936, p. 13.

"Chicagoan to Hold Series." *The Nashville Tennessean*, August 1, 1935, p. 6.

"Chief Detective Returns." *The Nashville Tennessean*, August 18, 1923, p. 3.

"Child Loses in Race with Death." *The Nashville Tennessean*, January 7, 1935, p. 1.

"Chesapeake & Nashville Changes Hands." *The Nashville American*, September 30, 1905.

"Chile con Carne." *The Nashville Tennessean*, June 20, 1909, p. B 5.

"Chile con Carne." *The Nashville Tennessean*, and *The Nashville American*, October 2, 1910, p. C-6.

"Chile con Carne." *The Nashville Tennessean*, September 4, 1910, p. A-9.

"Citizens Form Good Roads Club." *The Nashville Tennessean*, and *The Nashville American*, August 3, 1913, p. B-10.

"City Springs and Wells." *The Nashville American*, July 17, 1901, p. 8.

"Clarksville Bar Selects Acting County Judge." *The Nashville Tennessean*, August 15, 1929, p. 6.

"Classified." *The Nashville American*, April 19, 1908, p. 20.

"Classified." *The Nashville American*, June 16, 1901, p. 18.

"Cloyd Hotel Burns at Red Boiling Springs." *The Nashville Tennessean*, August 9, 1926, p. 5.

"Cloyd Place, Red Boiling Springs." *The Nashville American*, June 13, 1900, p. 8.

"Cloyd Place, or Upper Red Boiling Springs." *The Nashville American*, July 27, 1904, p. 10.

"Cloyd Place, or Upper Red Boiling Springs." *The Nashville American*, June 15, 1904, p. 13.

Cloyd Place." *The Nashville Tennessean and The Nashville American*, July 14, p. B-8.

"Cloyd Place." *The Nashville Tennessean and The Nashville American*, September 20, 1916, p. 17.

"Club Notes." *The Nashville Tennessean*, July 27, 1939, p. 9.

"Club Officers Address Road Meeting." *The Nashville Tennessean*, June 26, 1927, p. 28.

"Club Representatives Attend Good Roads Dinner." *The Nashville Tennessean*, July 17, 1927, p. 2.

"Coalition Trio Visits Shelby." *The Nashville Tennessean*, June 28, 1938, pp. 1-2.

"Col. Henry Dickinson Tours Upper State to Boost Bonus Session." *The Nashville Tennessean*, April 26, 1932, p. 1-2.

"Columbia." *The Nashville Tennessean*, July 14, 1907, p. A-5.

"Come Straight to Cloyd Place." *The Nashville Tennessean and The Nashville American*, September 18, 1916, p. 11.

"Comfort Keynote at State Resort." *The Nashville Tennessean*, May 31, 1931, p. 24.

"Concentrated Herculean Water." *The Nashville Tennessean*, October 26, 1920, p. 5.

"Conference of Revenue Agents Here Tomorrow." *The Nashville Tennessean*, July 7, 1907, p. 5.

"Conference on Good Roads to Be Held Today." *The Nashville Tennessean*, November 21, 1927, p. 1.

"Consolidated Bus Lines." *The Nashville Tennessean*, May 4, 1941, p. 89.

"Consolidated Bus Line Terminal Opens June 1." *The Nashville Tennessean*, May 30, 1926, p. 1.

"Consolidated Lines." *The Nashville Tennessean*, July 25, 1939, p. 20.

"Construction to Commence Today on Peay Highway." *The Nashville Tennessean*, April 19, 1928." *The Nashville Tennessean*, pp. 1, 5.

"Contemplated Interurban Construction." *The Nashville Tennessean and The Nashville American*, April 16, 1912, p. 4.

"Contemplated Interurban Lines." *The Nashville Tennessean and The Nashville American*, August 4, 1912, p. 6.

"Cookeville Cage Meet Ends Today for Tenth District." *The Nashville Tennessean*, March 7, 1936, p. 7.

"Cookeville Rally Set for McCord." *The Nashville Tennessean*, September 28, 1944, p. 6.

"County Judge Reduces Hours for Open Court." *The Nashville Tennessean*, August 27, 1925, p. 3.

"Cooper Batteries." *The Nashville Tennessean*, June 23, 1921, p. B-4.

"County Court Sanctions Contract for Highway." *The Nashville Tennessean*, March 4, 1920, p. 9.

"Court Convenes." *The Nashville Tennessean*, March 13, 1938, p. 33.

"Creamery Men to Meet." *The Nashville Tennessean*, June 25, 1933, p. 10.

"Cumberland Motor Co. Gives Luncheon." *The Nashville Tennessean and The Nashville American*, November 28, 1915, D-1.

"Dairy Meeting." *The Nashville Tennessean*, June 20, 1935, p. 5.

"Dance at Red Boiling Springs Postponed." *The Nashville Tennessean*, June 18, 1932, p. 8.

"Dances." *The Nashville Tennessean*, July 21, 1936, p. 6.

"David Lipscomb Quartet to Mark Tour." *The Nashville Tennessean*, March 19, 1939, p. 11.

"Death Notices." *The Nashville Tennessean*, August 18, 1927, p. 5.

"Death Notices." *The Nashville Tennessean*, July 20, 1923, p. 16.

"Deaths of Tennesseans." *The Nashville American*, November 27, 1906, p. 6.

"Deliver Addresses at Red Boiling Springs." *The Nashville Tennessean*, April 7, 1918, p. 12.

"Deliveries on Star and Durant Steadily Growing." *The Nashville Tennessean*, April 29, 1923, p. 40.

"Democrats Announce Dates of Nominees to Election." *The Nashville Tennessean*, October 22, 1924, p. 8.

"Desolation After Flood in 4 Towns Awes Spectator." *The Nashville Tennessean*, January 2, 1927, p. 5

"Dickson." *The Nashville Tennessean*, October 28, 1923, p. 37.

"Doctors Will Meet Tuesday." *The Nashville Tennessean*, June 13, 1926, p. 32.

"Don't Quote Me." *The Nashville Tennessean*, June 16, 1940, p. 22.

Driver, C. C. "Red Boiling Springs." *The Nashville Tennessean*, February 3, 1924, p. 46.

Driver, C. C. "Red Boiling Springs." *The Nashville Tennessean*, February 17, 1924, p. 40.

Driver, C. C. "Red Boiling Springs." *The Nashville Tennessean*, February 10, 1924, p. 39.

Driver, C. C. "Red Boiling Springs." *The Nashville Tennessean*, January 20, 1924, p. 37.

Driver, C. C. "Red Boiling Springs." *The Nashville Tennessean*, March 9, 1924, p. 34.

Driver, C. C. "Red Boiling Springs." *The Nashville Tennessean*, March 16, 1924, p. 35.

Driver, C. C. "Red Boiling Springs." *The Nashville Tennessean*, March 2, 1924, p. 34.

"Divorce Suit." *The Nashville Tennessean*, and *The Nashville American*, September 23, 1911, p. 12.

"Dr. S. E. Gaines Heads Upper Cumberland Medicos." *The Nashville Tennessean*, June 28, 1931, p. 28.

"Donoho's Hotel." *The Nashville American*, July 12, 1905, p. 10.

"Double Line." *The Nashville American*, October 7, 1905, p. 6.

"Dolan Withdraws from Senate Race." *The Nashville Tennessean*, July 23, 1918, p. 12.

"Drink at Home and at Your Office." *The Nashville American*, August 2, 1901, p. 5.

"Dr. J. L. Goodnight Well Known C. P. Official, Dies." *The Nashville Tennessean and The Nashville American*, October 3, 1914, p. 8.

"Educational." *The Nashville Tennessean*, June 22, 1927, p. 12.

"Effeness Club." *The Nashville Tennessean*, August 12, 1940, p. 7.

"Effeness Club." *The Nashville Tennessean*, September 7, 1940, p. 12.

"8 Killed, 30 Hurt When Storm Hits Kentucky Town." *The Nashville Tennessean*, May 10, 1933, p. 1.

"18th District." *The Nashville Tennessean*, January 4, 1939, p. 9.

"Enjoy the Glorious 4th, 5th, 6th." *The Nashville Tennessean*, July 3, 1941, p. 6.

"Enrollment." *The Nashville Tennessean*, August 25, 1940, p. 16.

"Entertainer." *The Nashville Tennessean*, June 4, 1931, p. 3.

"Entertainments." *The Nashville American*, July 1, 1909, p. 7.

"Entertainment." *The Nashville American*, June 24, 1908, p. 5.

"Enthusiasm for Railway." *The Nashville American*, September 8, 1909, p. 5.

"Equalization Board to Meet Monday." The Nashville Tennessean, August 2, 1907, p. 7.

"Eskew Busy in Interest of Hotel Law Enforcement." *The Nashville Tennessean*, and *The Nashville American*, September 16, 1917, p. B-4.

"Eskew Reports on Hotel Work During Past Month." *The Nashville Tennessean*, and *The Nashville American*, August 6, 1916, p. B-11.

"Essex." *The Nashville Tennessean*, July 24, 1929, p. 7.

"Evidence of Prehistoric Man as Old as European Brother Sought in State." *The Nashville Tennessean*, September 7, 1926, p. 6.

"Extension of Lebanon Branch." *The Nashville American*, March 10, 1903, p. 5.

"Fair Visitor Dies in Route Home." *The Nashville Tennessean*, September 30, 1909, p .8.

"Fans Overflow in an Attempt to Watch Boxing Program." *The Nashville Tennessean*, January 12, 1935, p. 10.

"Fast Cage Games Played in 10th District Tourney." *The Nashville Tennessean*, February 27, 1937, p. 6.

"Favorites Reach Second Round in Most High Meets." *The Nashville Tennessean*, February 26, 1932, pp. 17-18.

Ferriss, Mary. "Trenton." *The Nashville Tennessean*, September 21, 1924, p. 38.

"File Suit." *The Nashville Tennessean*, February 19, 1936, p. 3.

Finney, Russel. "Nashville Day Livestock Fair Features Today." *The Nashville Tennessean*, September 16, 1930, pp. 1, 5.

"Fire Causes Heavy Loss at Red Boiling Springs." *The Nashville Tennessean*, January 3, 1929, p. 2.

"Firm to Build Brick Garage in Lafayette." *The Nashville Tennessean*, May 11, 1919, p. 4.

"Five Counties Propose Cross State Highway." *The Nashville Tennessean*, December 29, 1925, p. 14.

"Flee from Flood." *The Nashville Tennessean*, December 23, 1926, p. 5.

"Flippin-Glasgow Road, 20 Miles Asked Built." *The Nashville Tennessean*, December 11, 1925, p. 16.

"F. N. Boensch Jr. Passes Away." *The Nashville Tennessean*, July 3, 1918, p. 1.

Forbes, Charles B. "The Lay of the Land." *The Nashville Tennessean*, July 12, 1925, p. 4.

"For Everybody." *The Nashville Tennessean*, December 6, 1941, p. 12.

"Florence Merchant Will be Buried Today." *The Nashville Tennessean*, September 5, 1937, p. 3.

"Formal Opening Dance." *The Nashville Tennessean*, July 9, 1939, p. 4.

"Formal Opening Next Saturday June 9." *The Nashville Tennessean*, June 3, 1934, p. 22.

"Form Hotel Company." *The Nashville Tennessean*, September 23, 1929, p. 14.

"For Rent." *The Nashville Tennessean*, July 22, 1923, p. 31.

"Fourth District Carriers Meet." *The Nashville Tennessean*, May 31, 1931, p. 12.

"Fourth District Group Hear Mitchell." *The Nashville Tennessean*, May 31, 1932, p. 6.

"Franklin Mayor Will Not be a Candidate Again." *The Nashville Tennessean*, August 4, 1919, p. 7.

"Fraternal Organizations." *The Nashville Tennessean and The Nashville American*, November 19, 1916, p. B-7.

"Fine New Road in Trousdale." *The Nashville Tennessean*, August 22, 1908, p. 3.

"For Building a Run Down Constitution." *The Nashville American*, August 6. 1901, p. 5.

"Foreclosure Bill." *The Nashville American*, January 4, 1906, p. 6.

"Ford Sales." *The Nashville Tennessean and The Nashville American*, March 2, 1913, p. 9 B-1.

"For Pike Here to Red Boiling Springs." *The Nashville Tennessean and The Nashville American*, January 8, 1914, p. 14.

"For Sale for Division or Rent." *The Nashville American*, March 10, 1903, p. 5.

"For Sale or Rent." *The Nashville Tennessean and The Nashville American*, April 20, 1913, p. A-8.

"For Sale." *The Nashville American*, August 17, 1902, p. 19.

"Fox-Robinson Wedding Ceremony is Quiet Event." *The Nashville Tennessean*, June 13, 1926, p. 34.

"Frank Davis." *The Nashville Tennessean*, July 31, 1908, p. 8.

"Full Explanation." *The Nashville American*, August 11, 1901, p. 13.

"Gallatin Editor is Elected Head of State Press." *The Nashville Tennessean*, June 20, 1937, p. 8.

"Gallatin to Dixon Springs." *The Nashville American*, July 31, 1909, p. 2.

Gammon, CL. *Murder, Mayhem, and Moonshine: True Macon County Crime Stories*. Lafayette, Tennessee: Deep Read Press, 2022, pp. 168-181.

Gammon, CL. *Revenue Raiders: Macon County's Whiskey War*. Lafayette, Tennessee: Deep Read Press, 2022, pp. 76-77.

Gammon, CL. *The Fountain of Youth at Red Boiling Springs, Tennessee, Part 1*. Lafayette, Tennessee: Deep Read Press, 2024, pp. 65-66, 88, 91-92, 163-164.

"Gathered in Hotel Lobbies." *The Nashville American*, August 1, 1908, p. 3.

"Get Ready for Winter Now." *The Nashville Tennessean*, October 3, 1925, p. 4.

"Given $5,000 Verdict." *The Nashville Tennessean*, June 8, 1934, p. 5.

"Go by Bus." *The Nashville Tennessean*, December 10, 1934, p. 6.

"Goes on Vacation." *The Nashville Tennessean*, July 26, 1928, p. 1.

"Goes to Red Boiling. *The Nashville Tennessean and The Nashville American*, August 4, 1912, p. A-8.

"Golden Gloves Entry List." *The Nashville Tennessean*, January 21, 1940, p. 38.

"Gone to Red Boiling Springs." *The Nashville American*, May 23, 1903, p. 10.

"Good Road Men Adopt Highway Commission Plan." *The Nashville Tennessean*, April 5, 1929, pp. 1, 5.

"Good Roads Lead to Summer Resorts Near Nashville." *The Nashville Tennessean*, August 4, 1925, p. 5.

"Good Roads Meeting at the Board of Trade." *The Nashville Tennessean*, and *The Nashville American*, July 26, 1913, p. 3.

"Good Roads Meeting." *The Nashville Tennessean*, and *The Nashville American*, July 24, 1913, p. 4.

"Good Railroad Territory." *The Nashville American*, May 23, 1905, p. 4.

"Good Work at Red Boiling Springs." *The Nashville Tennessean and The Nashville American*, June 28, 1914, p. D-3.

"Go To Red Boiling Springs by Bus." *The Nashville Tennessean*, June 11, 1933, p. 2.

"Governor Alf Taylor." *The Nashville Tennessean*, October 20, 1922, p. 4.

"Governor's Veto Again Overridden." *The Nashville American*, February 4, 1909, p. 1.

"Governor to Speak at Carthage Saturday." *The Nashville Tennessean*, July 4, 1927, p. 10.

"Graduates Hold Perfect Record of Attendance." *The Nashville Tennessean*, May 2, 1943, p. 45.

Grimsley, Will. "Biggest to Littlest, Every Eager Golden Glover Admits (Not Bashfully) He's Sure to Win Title." *The Nashville Tennessean*, January 31, 1939, p. 10.

"Guests at Springs Celebrate Victory." *The Nashville Tennessean*, July 25, 1918, p. 14.

"Guests Escape in their Nightclothes." *The Nashville Tennessean and The Nashville American*, August 28, 1915, p. 7.

"Gun Club Formed at Red Boiling Springs." *The Nashville Tennessean*, August 7, 1927, p. 7.

Hannon, Michael. "Scopes Trial (1925)." University of Minnesota Law School, 2010, p. 18.

"Harned Speaks Before Teachers Institute." *The Nashville Tennessean*, June 28, 1923, p. 6.

"Harry W. Smith." *The Nashville Tennessean and The Nashville American*, September 14, 1915, p. 2.

"Head Funeral Held." *The Nashville Tennessean*, August 25, 1933, p. 8.

"Head of Black Waters." *The Nashville Tennessean and The Nashville American*, February 16, p. B-5.

"Heavy Damage Done by Rain in City and State." *The Nashville Tennessean*, December 22, 1926, pp. 1, 5.

"Heavy Travel Keeps Up." *The Nashville, Tennessean*, July 7, 1907, p. 20.

"He Denies any Wrongdoing." *The Nashville American*, March 24, 1908, p. 2.

"Her Only Hope." *The Nashville American*, September 1, 1901. p. 3.

"Here's How They Faired in Gloves." *The Nashville Tennessean*, January 31, 1942, p. 22.

"High Tax Deal Truckers' Offer." *The Nashville Tennessean*, February 15, 1939, pp. 1, 8.

"Highway to be Built. *The Nashville Tennessean*, February 18, 1925, p. 14.

"Highway to Red Boiling Springs." *The Nashville Tennessean*, and *The Nashville American*, July 26, 1913, p. 4.

"Hilarity Reigns as Shriners Invade Red Boiling Springs." *The Nashville Tennessean*, June 21, 1936, p. 7.

"Hill Cut Down to Save Seven Miles Road Work." *The Nashville Tennessean*, August 7, 1927, p. 24.

"Hix-Johnson." *The Nashville Tennessean*, and *The Nashville American*, October 27, 1911, p. 5.

"Holiday Enjoyed as Nashville Observes Sane Fourth of July," *The Nashville Tennessean*, July 5, 1934, pp. 1-2.

"Honks of Nashville Auto Club." *The Nashville Tennessean*, April 9, 1922, p. B-4.

"Honks of Nashville Auto Club." *The Nashville Tennessean*, August 20, 1922, p. C-1.

"Honks of Nashville Auto Club." *The Nashville Tennessean*, June 25, 1922, p. C-2.

"Hooper to Speak Here for Republican Party." *The Nashville Tennessean*, October 10, 1924, p. 22.

"Hopkins Speaking Dates Announced." *The Nashville Tennessean*, September 18, 1928, p. 2.

"Horton and 5,000 Others to Honor Peay in Road Meet Today." *The Nashville Tennessean*, May 2, 1928, p. 10.

"Horton, Others Invited to Highway Meeting." *The Nashville Tennessean*, June 1, 1930, p. 5.

"Horton Received by Large Crowd to Dedicate Road." *The Nashville Tennessean*, May 6, 1928, p. 5.

"Hotel Destroyed by Fire." *The Nashville Tennessean and The Nashville American*, February 17, 1912, p. 5.

"Hotel Man Dies." *The Nashville Tennessean*, June 17, 1932, p. 10.

"Hotel News and General Notes." *The Nashville American*, May 7, 1903, p. 2.

"Hotels at Red Boiling Springs Draw $10 Fines." *The Nashville Tennessean*, and *The Nashville American*, August 26, 1917, p. B-1.

"Houses-Furnished." *The Nashville Tennessean*, June 24, 1925, p. 15.

"Hudson's Great 8." *The Nashville Tennessean*, April 13, 1930, p. 76.

"Huge Caravan Being Planned for Al Menah." *The Nashville Tennessean*, June 3, 1936, pp. 1, 2.

"'Husk' O'Hare and His Band." *The Nashville Tennessean*, July 24, 1931, p. 11.

"Huntingdon." *The Nashville Tennessean*, July 9,1922, p. A-6.

"Injuries Feared Fatal." *The Nashville Tennessean*, September 9, 1936, p. 5.

"Improved Facilities at Watering Place." *The Nashville Tennessean*, and *The Nashville American*, July 21, 1916, p. 5.

"Indications Point to a Very Large Attendance." *The Nashville American*, September 16, 1909, p. A-18.

"Institute in Progress at Red Boiling Springs." *The Nashville Tennessean*, June 28, 1922, p. 12.

"Interest in C & N Ownership." *The Nashville American*, October 4, 1905, p. 4.

"Investments." *The Nashville Tennessean*, April 14, 1940, p. 45.

"I. O. O. F. Birthplace." *The Nashville American*, March 12, 19004, p. 10.

"Ira Harman Now on Honeymoon." *The Nashville Tennessean and The Nashville American*, August 8, 1915, p. C-9.

Isaacson, Doris. *Maine: A Guide Down East.* Rockland, Maine: *Courier-Gazette*, Inc., 1970, p. 398.

"Jackson County." *The Nashville Tennessean*, and *The Nashville American*, December 17, 1911, p. B-17.

"James L. Sloan." *The Nashville American*, August 27, 1906, p. 5.

"Jeff L. Stafford, 70, Was a Native of Lincoln County." *The Nashville Tennessean*, June 10, 1925, p. 14.

"Jesse Gore." *The Nashville American*, June 24, 1908, p. 7.

"John W. Morton, Jr." *The Nashville American*, August 16, 1908, p. 24.

"Jollity Club at Red Boiling Springs, *The Nashville Tennessean*, and *The Nashville American*, August 13, 1916, p. 7.

"Judge Baker." *The Nashville American*, August 18, 1908, p. 4.

"Judge Hull Speaks at Blooming Springs." *The Nashville Tennessean*, October 29, 1922, p. 4.

"Judge Lansden is Rapidly Improving." *The Nashville Tennessean and The Nashville American*, August 22, 1914, p. 9.

"Jungermann's." *The Nashville Tennessean and The Nashville American*, September 30, 1916, p. 4.

"Junior Woodmen to Meet." *The Nashville Tennessean*, March 19, 1945, p. 2.

"J. W. Bean Heads Carrier Group." *The Nashville Tennessean*, July 6, 1941, p. 5.

Keith, Jeanette. In *Rural Life and Culture in the Upper Cumberland*. Lexington, Kentucky: University of Kentucky Press, 2004, pp. 178-195.

"Kentucky and Cumberland River, *The Nashville American*, July 26, 1905, p. 5.

"Kentucky Dog Leads Fox Hunt." *The Nashville Tennessean*, October 9, 1928, p. 2.

"Knights Columbús Presents Charity Show Here Monday." *The Nashville Tennessean*, December 12, 1936, p. 8.

"Known for Hospitality." *The Nashville Tennessean*, July 23, 1933, p. 11.

"Knoxville Bus Terminal Approved." *The Nashville Tennessean*, November 20, 1929, p. 9.

"Labor Day Celebration. August 31, 1935, p. 11.

"Lack of Interest." *The Nashville American*, August 4, 1904, p. 2.

"Lafayette Basketeers Defeat Red Boiling Springs." *The Nashville Tennessean*, February 19, 1924, p. 7.

"Lafayette Legion Sponsors Boxing." *The Nashville Tennessean*, July 6, 1935, p. 9.

"Lafayette Picked for School Site." *The Nashville Tennessean*, October 12, 1926, p. 9.

"Lafayette Quint Has Won Six Straight Games." *The Nashville Tennessean*, February 20, 1924, p 11.

"Large Hotel to be Built at Red Boiling Springs." *The Nashville Tennessean*, September 7, 1919, p. A-7.

"Lands and Farms for Sale." *The Nashville Tennessean*, February 27, 1924, p. 13.

"Leading Hotels and Cafes." *The Nashville Tennessean*, June 15, 1924, p. 36.

"Legionnaires Celebrate." *The Nashville Tennessean*, September 6, 1932, p. 12.

Lewis, Frank W. "Political." *The Nashville Tennessean*, June 1, 1909, p. 4.

"Line Up for Normal Game is Selected." *The Nashville Tennessean*, September 28, 1920, p. 2.

"Lipscomb Cagers Engage Martin." *The Nashville Tennessean*, November 25, 1942, p. 11.

"Lipscomb High Tops Red Boiling Springs." *The Nashville Tennessean*, January 18, 1942, p. 42.

"Listen to This." *The Nashville American*, June 13, 1909, p. 4.

"Literary League Meeting is Set." *The Nashville Tennessean*, March 25, 1938, p. 20.

"Local Physicians Plan to Attend Conference." *The Nashville Tennessean*, June 2, 1929, p. 12.

"Lost." *The Nashville Tennessean*, November 14, 1923, p. 14.

"Lost Silver Mine." *The Nashville American*, November 5, 1905, p. 8.

"Louisville and Nashville Railroad Summer Excursion Fares." *The Nashville Tennessean*, May 14, 1919, p. 4.

"Loungers of the Lobby." *The Nashville American*, August 28, 1909, p. 4.

"Lowe Boosts Red Boiling Springs Road." *The Nashville Tennessean*, and *The Nashville American*, September 14, 1913, p. D-8.

"Low Summer Fares." *The Nashville Tennessean*, June 15, 1924, p. 5.

"Low Summer Tourist Fares." *The Nashville Tennessean*, June 9, 1923, p. 8.

"Low Weekend Fares." *The Nashville Tennessean*, June 16, 1925, p. 2.

"Lumber." *The Nashville Tennessean*, October 28, 1935, p. 10.

"Macon County Boasts." *The Nashville American*, April 18, 1905, p. 5.

"Macon County May Secure Railroad Line. *The Nashville Tennessean*, and *The Nashville American*, March 31, 1916, p. 7.

"Macon County to Aid Red Cross Work." *The Nashville Tennessean and The Nashville American*, July 31, 1917, p. 3.

"Macon County to Hold Livestock Week." *The Nashville Tennessean*, October 24, 1927, p. 2.

"Macon Farmers to Grow More Tobacco." *The Nashville Tennessean*, February 8, 1924, p. 6.

"M'Alister Appoints New R. F. C. Committee." *The Nashville Tennessean*, February 12, 1933, p. 2.

"Manager." *The Nashville Tennessean*, June 4, 1933, p. 5.

"Many Charters Granted Thursday." *The Nashville Tennessean*, May 21, 1909, p. 3.

"Many Popular Resorts." *The Nashville American*, May 29, 1901, p. 6.

"Many Resort Hotels are O.K. Says Bolton." *The Nashville Tennessean*, July 21, 1923, p. 5.

"Many Speakers to be at Peay Road Meeting." *The Nashville Tennessean*, August 31, 1928, p. 4.

"May Build Railroad Line in Macon County." April 5, 1916, p. 7.

"McClellan." *The Nashville Tennessean*, February 28, 1929, p. 9.

"Medicinal Water." *The Nashville American*, August 15, 1901, p. 15.

"Medicos Meet Today." *The Nashville Tennessean*, June 6, 1934, p. 8.

"Meeting Called of Mysterious Order." *The Nashville Tennessean and The Nashville American*, May 24, 1915, p. 10.

"Meeting Tonight of the United Snipe Hunters." *The Nashville Tennessean and The Nashville American*, May 25, 1915, p. 12.

"Meets Next Friday." *The Nashville American*, June 18, 1904, p. 6.

"Member of Brigade is Killed in Kentucky in Kentucky Accident." *The Nashville Tennessean*, May 21, 1938, p. 2.

"Members of the State Draft Board." *The Nashville Tennessean*, October 17, 1940, p. 11.

"Memorial Service." *The Nashville Tennessean*, July 31, 1925, p. 2.

"Middle Tennessee and its Resources." *The Nashville Tennessean and The Nashville American*, July 15, 1917, C-1.

"Midstate District Tourneys." *The Nashville Tennessean*, February 21, 1945, p. 9.

"Minor Notes." *The Nashville American*, May 15, 1901, p. 3.

"Mitchell Says Victory Ahead." *The Nashville Tennessean*, July 19, 1938, p. 8.

"Mitchell Speaking Dates This Week Announced." *The Nashville Tennessean*, July 5, 1942, 5.

"Modern Hotel at Red Boiling Springs, *The Nashville Tennessean*, and *The Nashville American*, July 29, 1916, p. 12.

"Montgomery Sport Scribe Marries Here." *The Nashville Tennessean*, and *The Nashville American*, August 9, 1916, p. 12.

"More Joint Debates." *The Nashville American*, August 17, 1904, p. 3.

"More Evacuation Expected Here." *The Nashville Tennessean*, January 3, 1943, p. 1.

"More than 15,000 Bottles!" *The Nashville Tennessean*, April 11, 1926, p. 4.

"More than 150 Fights to be Held in Golden Gloves Meet." *The Nashville Tennessean*, February 3, 1935, p. 12.

"Morgan Sees Farms as Miners' Hope, He Tells Press Section." *The Nashville Tennessean*, July 7, 1933, p. 1.

Morrow, Jr., Henry. "Road Project Endorsed in Macon." *The Nashville Tennessean*, and *The Nashville American*, August 2, 1913, p. 1.

"Mother of Show Truck Victim Sought." *The Nashville Tennessean*, September 23, 1926, p. 2.

"Movement to Build New Railroad Line, *The Nashville Tennessean*, and *The Nashville American*, March 16, 1906, p. A-7.

"Mr. Morton Recovering." *The Nashville American*, July 4, 1908, p. 5.

"Mrs. Alice Capshaw." *The Nashville Tennessean*, July 15, 1932, p. 16.

"Mrs. Benton McMillin Completes Organization of Democratic Women." *The Nashville Tennessean*, October 6, 1924, p. 12.

"Mrs. Frank M. Davis." *The Nashville American*, August 5, 1907, p. 2.

"Mrs. Jacob Walker, Bass, Alabama." *The Nashville American*, August 4, 1909, p. 2.

"Mrs. James L. Sloan." *The Nashville American*, June 30, 1906, p. 6.

"Mrs. Myrtle W. Jordan." *The Nashville Tennessean and The Nashville American*, Jue 23, 1915, p. 76.

"Musical Equipment." *The Nashville Tennessean* August 6, 1938, p. 11.

"Nashville Autoist Arrested in Macon." *The Nashville Tennessean*, and *The Nashville American*, July 30, 1913, p. 2.

"Nashville Bends to Repair Task After Drenching." *The Nashville Tennessean*, June 30, 1928, pp. 1, 20.

"Nashville Boosters Making Plans for their Twenty-first Visitation." *The Nashville Tennessean*, May 10, 1931, p. 10.

"Nashville on the Firing Line." *The Nashville Tennessean*, July 19, 1925, p. 35.

"Nashville's 1926-1927 Radio Season Opens Monday September 6." *The Nashville Tennessean*, September 5, 1926, p. 6.

"Naturopathists Elect Officers." *The Nashville Tennessean*, November 6, 1938, p. 7.

"NBC Artist." *The Nashville Tennessean*, May 31, 1932, p. 9.

"Negro Runs Amok." *The Nashville American*, August 19, 1908, p. 7.

"New Business Opened in Nashville Just for Your Health's Sake." *The Nashville Tennessean*, July 15, 1928, p 13.

"New Electric Line." *The Nashville American*, August 29, 1906, p 3.

"New Hotel Planned for Red Boiling Springs." *The Nashville Tennessean*, February 10, 1924, p. 24.

"News Notes from the Lodges." *The Nashville American*, June 15, 1907, p. 7.

"News of the City Briefly Told." *The Nashville Tennessean*, June 24, 1921, p. 8.

"News of City Briefly Told." *The Nashville Tennessean*, May 14, 1921, p. 4.

"News of Railroads." *The Nashville American*, June 5, 1903, p. 7.

"New State Road for Macon Planned." *The Nashville Tennessean*, March 2, 1926, p. 2.

"New Travelers with J. S. Reeves and Company." *The Nashville Tennessean and The Nashville American*, January 11, 1914, p. C-14.

"New Trolley Line." *The Nashville American*, March 23, 1906, p. 2.

"1939 Golden Gloves Roster." *The Nashville Tennessean*, January 22, 1939, p. 14.

"Nixon Battles Lewis Tonight." *The Nashville Tennessean*, January 31, 1942, p. 22.

"Nominating Body is Appointed by Hotel Men." *The Nashville Tennessean*, April 23, 1929, pp. 1, 5.

"No More Rain Forecast; River Continues Fall." *The Nashville Tennessean*, January 9, 1943, p. 1.

"No Opposition to Appropriation for Law Enforcement. *The Nashville Tennessean and The Nashville American*, March 30, 1913, p. 10.

"No Selection Made." *The Nashville American*, August 18, 1904, p. 5.

"Notes of the Trade." *The Nashville American*, October 8, 1909, p. 6.

"Now Open – Palace Hotel." *The Nashville Tennessean, The Nashville Tennessean*, May 6, 1934, p. 20.

"Numerous Cures at Red Boiling." *The Nashville Tennessean*, July 18, 1932, p. 5.

"Obituary Notes." *The Nashville American*, March 24, 1900, p. 2.

"Obituary." *The Nashville Tennessean*, and *The Nashville American*, June 26, 1911, p. 4.

"Officials Give Out Statement." The Nashville Tennessean, June 6, 1907, p. 9.

"O'Hare Orchestra Plays at Red Boiling Springs." *The Nashville Tennessean*, May 31, 1931, p. 37.

"O. M. Adams is Buried at Cookeville Sunday, *The Nashville Tennessean*, August 24, 1936, p. 3.

"On Vacation." *The Nashville Tennessean*, August 30, 1932, p. 2.

"Open for Season Now." *The Nashville Tennessean*, and *The Nashville American*, May 6, 1916, p. 9.

"Open for the Season." *The Nashville Tennessean*, June 15, 1933, p. 2.

"Opening Dance." *The Nashville Tennessean*, May 29, 1931, p. 10.

"Opening." *The Nashville Tennessean*, June 14, 1942, p. 52.

"Opening." *The Nashville Tennessean*, May 25, 1937, p. 2.

"Operation Successful." *The Nashville American*, August 14, 1906, p. 7.

"Obtain Light System." *The Nashville Tennessean*, October 12,1924, p. 6.

"Opening Announcement." *The Nashville Tennessean*, June 16, 1928, p. 7.

"Options Taken on Large Areas of Macon for Oil." *The Nashville Tennessean*, September 7, 1919, p. A-7.

"Otis Parkhurst." *The Nashville Tennessean*, January 7, 1922, p. 12.

"Out of Town Society." *The Nashville American*, June 23, 1908, p. 7.

"Out of Town Weddings. *The Nashville Tennessean and The Nashville American*, November 12, 1914, p. 12.

"Owners, New Buyers, Prospects Call it Value of Values." *The Nashville Tennessean*, April 27, 1930, p. 8.

"Palace Hotel." *The Nashville Tennessean*, August 31, 1940, p. 10.

"Palace Hotel." *The Nashville Tennessean*, July 1, 1938, p. 20.

"Palace Hotel." *The Nashville Tennessean*, June 4, 1933, p. 2.

"Palace Hotel." *The Nashville Tennessean*, June 19, 1921, p. 9.

"Palace Hotel." *The Nashville Tennessean*, June 1, 1930, p. 3.

"Palace Hotel." *The Nashville Tennessean*, June 16, 1943, p. 11.

"Palace Hotel." *The Nashville Tennessean*, June 20, 1945, p. 9.

"Past Grand Master." *The Nashville American*, August 13, 1906, p. 5.

"Patents for Southerners." *The Nashville American*, April 14, 1905, p. 11.

"Pathé." *The Nashville Tennessean*, November 30, 1919, p. 12.

"Peay Road Group to be Chartered." *The Nashville Tennessean*, September 2, 1928, p. 12.

"Peay Road Group Will Meet Friday." *The Nashville Tennessean*, August 24, 1931, p. 2.

"Peay will Get G.O.P. Votes, Says Sheperd." *The Nashville Tennessean*, August 21, 1922, p. 3.

"Peeler Recuperating." *The Nashville Tennessean*, August 25, 1996, p. 2.

"Perry to be Speaker at Peay Road Meet Today." *The Nashville Tennessean*, September 1, 1928, p. 11.

"Personal Mention and Brief Bits of Personal News." *The Nashville American*, September 18, 1909, p. 5.

"Personal Mention." *The Nashville American*, August 1, 1908, p. 6.

"Personal Mention." *The Nashville American*, July 9, 1907, p. 7.

"Personal Mention." *The Nashville American*, June 19, 1907, p. 10.

"Personal Mention." *The Nashville American*, June 23, 1907, p. 20.

"Personal Mention." *The Nashville Tennessean*, July 15, 1934, p. 17.

"Personal Mention." *The Nashville Tennessean*, July 7, 1940, p. 23.

"Personal Notes." *The Nashville American*, August 26, 1910, p. 5.

"Personal Notes." *The Nashville American*, May 20, 1906, p. 21.

"Personal Notes." *The Nashville Tennessean*, May 20, 1909, p. 5.

"Personal, Political and Hotel Gossip." *The Nashville Tennessean*, and *The Nashville American*, May 19, 1911, p. 7.

"Personal, Political and Hotel Gossip." *The Nashville Tennessean*, and *The Nashville American*, July 18, 1911, p. 10.

"Personal, Political and Hotel Gossip." *The Nashville Tennessean*, and *The Nashville American*, October 19, 1911, p. 12.

"Personals." *The Nashville Tennessean and The Nashville American*, August 24, 1914, p. 5.

"Personals." *The Nashville Tennessean*, and *The Nashville American*, July 21, 1911, p. 5.

Personals." *The Nashville Tennessean*, and *The Nashville American*, November 4, 1911, p. 5.

"Personals." *The Nashville Tennessean and The Nashville American*, September 28, 1914, p. 5.

"Personals." *The Nashville Tennessean*, September 8, 1908, p. 5.

"Pike Hartsville to Red Boiling Springs." *The Nashville Tennessean*, and *The Nashville American*, July 24, 1913, p. 5.

"Plan First Convention." *The Nashville Tennessean*, and *The Nashville American*, July 9, 1911, p. A-6.

"Plan Railroad to Red Boiling Springs." *The Nashville Tennessean*, and *The Nashville American*, February 27, 1916, p. 10-A.

"Political News at Headquarters." *The Nashville Tennessean*, October 17, 1920, p. A-3.

"Power Firm Gets Permit to Cut Rates One-Tenth." *The Nashville Tennessean*, September 21, 1929, p. 1.

"Policemen at the Springs." *The Nashville American*, July 11, 1910, p. 2.

"Political Gossip and Hotel News." *The Nashville American*, August 23, 1910, p. 4.

"Political Gossip and Hotel News." *The Nashville American*, August 24, 1909, p. 4.

"Political Gossip and Hotel News." *The Nashville American*, July 15, 1910, p. 4.

"Political News & Personal Notes." *The Nashville American*, August 17, 1902, p. 8.

"Political News & Personal Notes." *The Nashville American*, August 22, 1902, p. 8.

Political News & Personal Notes." *The Nashville American*, September 8, 1902, p. 2.

"Political Notes and Hotel Gossip." *The Nashville American*, August 14, 1905, p. 4.

"Political Notes and Hotel Gossip." *The Nashville American*, July 28, 1906, p. 5.

"Political Notes and Hotel Gossip." *The Nashville American*, September 7, 1904, p. 8.

"Political Notes and Hotel Gossip." *The Nashville American*, September 24, 1904, p. 3.

"Pope, At Clarksville, Draws Record Crowd; Visits Sumner, Macon." *The Nashville Tennessean*, July 28, 1932, p. 1.

"Power Groups Seek New Dam." *The Nashville Tennessean*, June 10, 1938, p. 10.

"Power Line Extended." *The Nashville Tennessean*, July 15, 1924, p. 3.

"Pretty Weddings at Cowan." *The Nashville Tennessean and The Nashville American*, June 10, p A-8.

"Prices Reduced." *The Nashville Tennessean*, August 31, 1930, p. 2.

Priest, J. Percy. "McAlister Fails to Show Jackson Good Roads Evil." *The Nashville Tennessean*, July 3, 1928, pp. 1, 5.

Priest, J. Percy. "Nameless Highways May Lead to Places of Interest." *The Nashville Tennessean*, April 21, 1940, p. 14.

Priest, J. Percy. "Politics." *The Nashville Tennessean*, July 26, 1928, p. 1.

"Priest Makes Plea for Unity." *The Nashville Tennessean*, October 24, 1940.

"Private Institutions of Learning in Tennessee." *The Nashville Tennessean*, September 8, 1907, p. D-2.

"Programmes and Hostesses at the Women's." *The Nashville American*, September 30, 1906, B-15.

"Proposed New Railroad." *The Nashville American*, September 3, 1907, p. 3.

"Pumpkintown is Hit by Hydrophobia Epidemic." *The Nashville Tennessean*, p. 14.

"P. T. A. Group Names Convention Delegates." *The Nashville Tennessean*, April 17, 1931, p. 1.

"Quicker Schedule to Red Boiling Springs." *The Nashville Tennessean and The Nashville American*, August 23, 1914, p. A-3.

"Railroad in Macon." *The Nashville Tennessean*, December 5, 1909, p. A-3.

"Railroad May Be Built to Red Boiling Springs." *The Nashville Tennessean*, September 18, 1909, p. 7.

"Railroad News, *The Nashville American*, August 12, 1905, p. 10.

"Railroad Planned in Macon County." *The Nashville American*, September 24, 1909, p. 13.

"Railroad Through Macon." *The Nashville American*, May 11, 1909, p. 12.

"Railroad to Red Boiling Springs." *The Nashville Tennessean*, January 26, 1910, p. 1.

"R & O Drug Company." *The Nashville Tennessean*, April 25, 1925, p. 16.

"Rank in File." *The Nashville Tennessean*, and *The Nashville American*, July 13, 1913, p. 20.

"Rank and File." *The Nashville Tennessean and The Nashville American*, July 4, 1915, p. C-2.

"Rank in File." *The Nashville Tennessean*, and *The Nashville American*, November 12, 1911, p. A-5.

"Rap Legislature at Road Meeting." *The Nashville Tennessean*, August 29, 1931, p. 12.

"Ready to Drive Away." *The Nashville Tennessean*, February 4, 1923, 33.

"Reception at the Palace Hotel." *The Nashville Tennessean and The Nashville American*, August 23, 1914, p. p. C-2.

"Receiver Named for Golf Course." *The Nashville Tennessean*, October 31, 1930, p. 18.

"Recruits Leave." *The Nashville Tennessean*, December 5, 1939, p. 14.

"Red Boiling, Cumberland Foothills, Provide Restful Atmosphere in Macon County." *The Nashville Tennessean*, September 10, 1937, p. 5.

"Red Boiling Springs Defeats Scottsville." *The Nashville Tennessean*, July 15, 1924, p. 6.

"Red Boiling Springs Celebrates Fourth." *The Nashville Tennessean*, July 6, 1918, p. 12.

"Red Boiling Springs Company Seeks Charter." *The Nashville Tennessean and The Nashville American*, March 17, 1917, p. 6.

"Red Boiling Springs Famous All Over the World, *The Nashville Tennessean*, August 4, 1932, p. 12.

"Red Boiling Springs High School Burns." *The Nashville Tennessean*, July 30, 1927, p. 1.

"Red Boiling Springs High School Opens Without Building." *The Nashville Tennessean*, September 30, 1927, p. 10.

"Red Boiling Springs Hotel." *The Nashville American*, April 6, 1904, p. 7.

"Red Boiling Springs Hotel." *The Nashville American*, July 24, 1904, p. 19.

"Red Boiling Springs Mecca for Many." *The Nashville Tennessean*, July 9, 1933, p. 16.

"Red Boiling Springs Popular." *The Nashville Tennessean*, August 19, 1932, p. 10.

"Red Boiling Springs Postmaster Nominated." *The Nashville Tennessean*, February 24, 1922, p. A-5.

"Red Boiling Springs Proves Popular Summer Resort." *The Nashville Tennessean*, July 24, 1932, p. 14.

"Red Boiling Springs Resort Awaits Upper Cumberland Doctors Today." *The Nashville Tennessean*, June 15, 1926, p. 8.

"Red Boiling Springs Schools to Close May 24." *The Nashville Tennessean*, May 23, 1929, p. 3.

"Red Boiling Springs Seeks New School." *The Nashville Tennessean*, May 2, 1928, p. 5.

"Red Boiling Springs." *The Nashville American*, August 12, 1900, p. 2.

"Red Boiling Springs." *The Nashville American*, August 19, 1900, p. 16.

"Red Boiling Springs." *The Nashville American*, August 25, 1904, p. 10.

"Red Boiling Springs." *The Nashville American*, August 5, 1900, p. 2.

"Red Boiling Springs." *The Nashville American*, July 20, 1901, p. 8.

"Red Boiling Springs." *The Nashville American*, June 9, 1901, p. 24.

"Red Boiling Springs." *The Nashville American*, May 18, 1909, p. 12.

"Red Boiling Springs." *The Nashville American*, May 25, 1906, p. 12.

"Red Boiling Springs." *The Nashville American*, November 5, 1905, p. 22.

"Red Boiling Springs." *The Nashville American*, September 9, 1903, p. 3.

"Red Boiling Springs, *The Nashville Tennessean and The Nashville American*, July 11, 1914, p. 3.

"Red Boiling Springs." *The Nashville Tennessean and The Nashville American*, July 15, 1915, p. B-4.

Red Boiling Springs." *The Nashville Tennessean*, and *The Nashville American*, July 20, 1913, p. C-4.

"Red Boiling Springs." *The Nashville Tennessean and The Nashville American*, June 19, 1915, p. 5.

"Red Boiling Springs." *The Nashville Tennessean*, and *The Nashville American*, May 4,1916, p. 5.

"Red Boiling Springs." *The Nashville Tennessean*, August 29, 1936, p. 5.

"Red Boiling Springs." *The Nashville Tennessean*, June 7, 1936, p. 19.

"Red Boiling Springs." *The Nashville Tennessean*, June 20, 1929, p. 19.

"Red Boiling Springs to Have Boxing July 30." *The Nashville Tennessean*, July 24, 1927, p. 10.

"Red Boiling Springs to Have New Bank Home." *The Nashville Tennessean*, September 29, 1927, p. 8.

"Red Boiling Springs Trims Scottsville." *The Nashville Tennessean*, August 6, 1927, p. 10.

"Red Boiling Springs Water." *The Nashville American*, July 30, 1901, p. 3.

"Red Boiling Springs Water." *The Nashville American*, June 23, 1901, p. 2.

"Red Boiling Springs Will Open Their Dance Season." *The Nashville Tennessean*, June 2, 1929, p. 39.

"Red Boiling Water." *The Nashville American*, My 18, 1902, p. 3.

"Red Cross Events at Red Boiling Springs, *The Nashville Tennessean*, August 25, 1918, p. A-6.

"Red Men." *The Nashville American*, June 30, 1906, p. 9.

"Red Springs to Have Road Meet." *The Nashville Tennessean*, August 16, 1928, p. 7.

"Reduced Bus Rates." *The Nashville Tennessean*, January 28, 1933, p. 8.

"Regret Expressed in Bus Ruling, *The Nashville Tennessean*, May 31, 1935, p. 3.

"Regitko Triumphs by Technical Kayo in Y Boxing Card." *The Nashville Tennessean*, January 22, 1935, p. 9.

"Rep. D. M. Coleman Out for Session." *The Nashville Tennessean*, October 26, 1937, p. 1.

"Request for Opinion." *The Nashville American*, August 28, 1904, p. 13.

"Reservations Being Made for Al Menah Trek to Red Boiling." *The Nashville Tennessean*, June 19, 1936, p. 15.

"Results of District Basketball Tourneys, College Meets." *The Nashville Tennessean*, March 1, 1940, p. 25.

"Ribbons Awarded Before Big Crowd at Smith Fair." *The Nashville Tennessean*, August 18, 1928, p. 5.

"River Excursions." *The Nashville Tennessean*, and *The Nashville American*, May 14, 1916, p. A-17.

"River Yields Body of Motorist Near Trousdale Ferry." *The Nashville Tennessean*, June 17, 1926, p. 1.

"Robert Kercheval Seriously Ill." *The Nashville American*, July 1, 1908, p. 10.

"Robert McEwen." *The Nashville American*, June 14, 1907, p. 3.

"Romantic Marriage of Mr. Thompson and Miss LeNeve. *The Nashville American*, September 20, 1910, p. 7.

"Round Trip from Nashville via Louisville & Nashville Railroad, *The Nashville Tennessean*, June 22, 1922, p. 7.

"Route Nashville to Red Boiling Springs." *The Nashville Tennessean and The Nashville American*, July 1, 1914, p. D-3.

"Rufus Lashlee." *The Nashville Tennessean and The Nashville American*, February 22, 1915, p. 5.

"Rumored Extension of Tennessee Central." *The Nashville American*, August 6, 1904, p. 2.

"Rural Churches Plan Prayers for Rain on 66th day of Drouth." *The Nashville Tennessean*, June 14, 1936, p. 1.

"Sale of International Trucks on the Increase." *The Nashville Tennessean*, November 11, 1923, p. 34.

"Sale of Red Boiling Springs." *The Nashville American*, September 22, 1905, p. 10.

"Sample Sale a Success." *The Nashville American*, March 16, 1906, p. 10.

"Samuel Henry." *The Nashville American*, October 15, 1906, p. 5.

"Sawmill Hand Injured at Red Boiling Springs." *The Nashville Tennessean*, August 25, 1922, p. 18.

"Scarlet Fever Closes School." *The Nashville Tennessean*, October 15, 1944, p. 42.

"School Highway Meet to Open." *The Nashville Tennessean*, June 23, 1927, p. 3.

Scott, Betty C. Meadows. *Macon County, Tennessee Obituaries and Articles, Volume 2*. Lafayette, Tennessee: Ridge Runner Publications, 2003, pp. 18, 21-22, 25, 47, 83, 85, 112.

Scott, Betty C. Meadows. *Macon County, Tennessee Obituaries and Articles, Volume 1*. Lafayette, Tennessee: Ridge Runner Publications, 2003, pp. 1, 4, 12, 25, 66, 68, 103, 107-108, 113, 136, 152, 171.

"'Scottsboro' Lawyer to Rest at Red Boiling Springs." *The Nashville Tennessean*, July 21, 1937, p. 3.

"Second Arrest Under New Law." *The Nashville American*, August 22, 1907, p. 3.

"Secure Option on Oil Well in Macon Co." *The Nashville Tennessean* and *The Nashville American*, October 7, 1910, p. 12.

"Senate Acts to Authorize 3 Bridges in Tennessee." *The Nashville Tennessean*, April 28, 1926, p. 1.

"Sensational Allegations." *The Nashville Tennessean* and *The Nashville American*, December 18, 1910, p. A-8.

"Sensational, Thrilling, Breathtaking." *The Nashville Tennessean*, September 29, 1938, p. 15.

"70¢ Value for Men 49¢." *The Nashville Tennessean*, November 23, 1923, p. 11.

"$7.15 Red Boiling Springs and Return." *The Nashville Tennessean*, June 23, 1923, p. 16.

"Shacklett-McQuiddy. *The Nashville Tennessean and The Nashville American*, June 27, 1912, p. 4.

"Sheriff Borum is on Vacation." *The Nashville Tennessean*, July 24, 1909, p. 10.

"'Shop by Telephone' Plans are Completed." *The Nashville Tennessean*, May 1, 1927, p. 15.

"Shot at Red Boiling Springs." *The Nashville Tennessean*, and *The Nashville American*, July 25, 1911, p. 4.

"Show Cause Order." *The Nashville Tennessean*, May 14, 1940, p. 4.

"Shrine Caravan Leaves June 20." *The Nashville Tennessean*, June 4, 1936, p. 1.

"Shropshire Lectures to Red Boiling Audience." *The Nashville Tennessean*, August 25, 1921, p. 8.

"Situations Wanted Male." *The Nashville Tennessean*, September 9, 1928, p. 24.

"$6.85 Red Boiling Springs and Return." *The Nashville Tennessean*, July 21, 1923, p. 3.

"$6.85 Red Boiling Springs and Return." *The Nashville Tennessean*, July 20, 1924, p. 10.

"$6.85 Red Boiling Springs." *The Nashville Tennessean*, May 21, 1922, p. 10.

"Sleet Does Heavy Damage Here But Relief Due Today." *The Nashville Tennessean*, March 20, 1934, p. 1.

"Smallpox is Prevalent in Macon County." *The Nashville Tennessean*, and *The Nashville American*, September 18, 1917, p. 7.

"Smith Countians on Institute Program." *The Nashville Tennessean*, May 31, 1924, p. 8.

"Snipe Hunters Elect Officers." *The Nashville Tennessean*, and *The Nashville American*, September 13, 1911, p. 12.

"Snipe Hunters to Meet Every Week." *The Nashville Tennessean and The Nashville American*, June 12, 1915, p. 5.

"Society." *The Nashville American*, March 6, 1908, p. 7.

"Society." *The Nashville American*, July 17, 1908, p. 7.

"Solons to Reunite at Red Boiling." *The Nashville Tennessean and The Nashville American*, August 14, 1917, p. 3.

"Southern Railroad Resorts." *The Nashville American*, February 17, 1906, p. 5.

"Speaking Dates of Austin Peay." *The Nashville Tennessean*, June 23, 1922, p. 3.

"Special Bus Rates Offered to Red Boiling Springs." *The Nashville Tennessean*, July 28, 1932, p. 6.

"Special Notice." *The Nashville Tennessean*, July 11, 1927, p. 2.

"Speeches are Set in Congress Race." *The Nashville Tennessean*, July 29, 1940, p. 3.

"Spend the Fourth of July at the New Cloyd Hotel." *The Nashville Tennessean*, July 30, 1929, p. 7.

"Spend Your Vacation on Cloyd Place." *The Nashville Tennessean*, July 8, 1920, p. 4.

"Spend Your Week of July 4th at the Palace Hotel." *The Nashville Tennessean*, June 27, 1937, p. 10.

"Spread of Automobile Lines." *The Nashville American*, August 26, 1909, p. 4.

"Spred is the Easy to Use Wall Paint." *The Nashville Tennessean*, May 8, 1945, p. 11.

"Springs to Carthage Road Work Underway." *The Nashville Tennessean*, December 17, 1926, p. 20.

"Staggering Blow Dealt Sam H. Borum." *The Nashville Tennessean*, August 14, 1909, p. 8.

"State Fox Hunt Meet to Open." *The Nashville Tennessean*, October 8, 1928, p. 12.

"State Health Officials Go to Red Boiling." *The Nashville Tennessean*, June 16, 1926, p. 2.

"State Preps." *The Nashville Tennessean*, January 24, 1942, p. 9.

"State Press Group is Asked to Join South's Publishers' Body." *The Nashville Tennessean*, July 7, 1933, p. 1.

"State Route No. 52." *The Nashville Tennessean*, November 9, 1924, p. 19.

"State's Progress in Schools-Roads Told." *The Nashville Tennessean*, June 25, 1927.

"State Treasurer's Semi-Annual Interest Report." *The Nashville Tennessean*, December 5, 1943, p. 45.

"State Treasurer's Semi-Annual Interest Report." *The Nashville Tennessean*, June 5, 1937, p. 9.

"State Treasurer's Semi-Annual Interest Report." *The Nashville Tennessean*, June 5, 1940, p. 20.

"Statistical Record." *The Nashville Tennessean*, and *The Nashville American*, September 10, 1916, p. 5.

"State Treasurer's Semi-Annual Interest Report." *The Nashville Tennessean*, December 5, 1930, p. 22.

"State Treasurer's Semi-Annual Interest Report." *The Nashville Tennessean*, December 5, 1928, p. 11.

"State Treasurer's Semi-Annual Interest Report." *The Nashville Tennessean*, December 5, 1923, p. 10.

"State Treasurer's Semi-Annual Interest Report." *The Nashville Tennessean*, December 5, 1924, p. 19.

"State Treasurer's Semi-Annual Interest Report." *The Nashville Tennessean*, December 5, 1922, p. 8.

"State Treasurer's Semi-Annual Interest Report." *The Nashville Tennessean*, June 5, 1938, p. 40.

"State Treasurer's Semi-Annual Interest Report." *The Nashville Tennessean*, June 5, 1939, p. 7.

"State Treasurer's Semi-Annual Interest Report." *The Nashville Tennessean*, June 5, 1925, p. 16.

"State Treasurer's Semi-Annual Interest Report." *The Nashville Tennessean*, June 5, 1924, p. 8.

"State Treasurer's Semi-Annual Interest Report." *The Nashville Tennessean*, June 5, 1923, p. 8.

"Statistical Record." *The Nashville Tennessean*, January 27, 1940, p. 11.

"Statistical Record." *The Nashville Tennessean*, June 6, 1918, p. 6.

"Statistical Record." *The Nashville Tennessean*, March 22, 1919, p. 7.

"State Board of Equalization." *The Nashville Tennessean*, July 27, 1907, p. 9.

"Statistical Record. *The Nashville Tennessean and The Nashville American*, April 11, 1914, p. 9.

Statistical Record." *The Nashville Tennessean and The Nashville American*, January 20, 1914, p. p. 2.

"Suffers Stroke." *The Nashville Tennessean*, July 13, 1933, p. 1.

"Suffrage Salmagundi." *The Nashville Tennessean and The Nashville American*, August 12, 1917, p. A-6.

Sulfur Measurements Handbook. Calgary, Canada: Galvanic Applied Sciences, Inc., 2001.

"Summer Excursion Fares." *The Nashville Tennessean*, June 6, 1921, p. 2.

"Summer Rates to Red Boiling Springs." *The Nashville Tennessean*, July 30, 1923, p. 5.

"Summer Rates to Red Boiling Springs." *The Nashville Tennessean*, June 29, 1923, p. 5.

"Summer Resorts." *The Nashville American*, June 13, 1908, p. 10.

"Summer Resorts." *The Nashville American*, June 15, 1906, p. 12.

"Summer Resorts." *The Nashville American*, May 16, 1903, p. 7.

"Summer School." *The Nashville Tennessean*, June 28, 1940, p. 23.

"Summons Comes to "Bob" M'Ewan." *The Nashville Tennessean and The Nashville American*, October 24, 1916, p. 1.

"Sumner Sheriff is Injured in Auto Upset." *The Nashville Tennessean*, September 14, 1931, p. 3.

"Tacky Party Given for Red Cross Fund." *The Nashville Tennessean, and The Nashville American*, August 17, 1917, p. 2.

"Tanlac Agencies." *The Nashville Tennessean and The Nashville American*, September 5, 1915, p. A-7.

"Teachers' Chautauqua Opens at Red Boiling Springs." *The Nashville Tennessean*, June 27,

"Teachers' Institute Declared a Success." *The Nashville Tennessean*, June 24, 1923, p. 12.

"Teachers' Institute to be Held Red Boiling Springs." *The Nashville Tennessean*, June 16, 1922, p. 4.

"Teachers Will Meet." *The Nashville Tennessean*, June 18, 1923, p. 12.

"Telephone In Macon County." *The Nashville American*, April 3, 1909, p. 4.

"10 Cents a Pint." *The Nashville American*, June 15, 1902, p. 15.

"Tennessee Airlines is Issued Charter." *The Nashville Tennessean*, June 1, 1944, p. 3..

"Tenth District Pairings Given." *The Nashville Tennessean*, February 25, 1936, p. 14.

"Tennessee Central R.R." *The Nashville American,* June 10, 1903, p. 10.

"Tennessee Health Food Co. *The Nashville Tennessean,* June 23, 1928, p. 31.

"Tennessee Press." *The Nashville Tennessean,* October 27, 1926, p. 4.

"Tennessee State Fair Department." *The Nashville American,* September 3, 1906, p. 6.

"Tennessee." *The Nashville American,* June 29, 1901, p. 9.

"Tenth District Juniors Open Meet on Tuesday." *The Nashville Tennessean,* February 23, 1937, p. 9.

"Tenth District Pairings Given." *The Nashville Tennessean,* February 25, 1936, p. 14.

"That Railroad Survey." *The Nashville Tennessean and The Nashville American,* September 3, 1912, p. 6.

"The Importance of Drinking Pure Water!" *The Nashville American,* April 8, 1900, p. 12.

"The Interurban and the Market." *The Nashville Tennessean and The Nashville American,* February 22, 1913, p. 6.

"The New Cloyd Hotel." *The Nashville Tennessean,* July 1, 1928, p. 7.

"The New Palace Hotel." *The Nashville Tennessean and The Nashville American,* June 18, 1914, p. 10.

"The Old Original Red Boiling Springs." *The Nashville American,* May 26, 1905, p. 12.

"The Old Reliable Red Boiling Springs." *The Nashville American,* June 7, 1900, p. 8.

"The Palace Hotel." *The Nashville Tennessean and The Nashville American,* May 24, 1917, p. 9.

"The Palace Hotel." *The Nashville Tennessean*, July 8, 1932, p. 12.

"The Palace Hotel." *The Nashville Tennessean*, June 11, 1933, p. 2.

"The Palace Hotel." *The Nashville Tennessean*, June 22, 1944, p. 3,

"The Palace Hotel." *The Nashville Tennessean*, September 16, 1932, p. 15.

"The Palace Hotel." *The Nashville Tennessean*, September 2,1933, p. 5.

"The Personal Side." *The Nashville Tennessean*, June 13, 1925, p. 6.

"These are the Men Behind Veedol." *The Nashville Tennessean*, May 31, 1928, p. 5.

"These Boys Vie in Gloves." *The Nashville Tennessean*, January 26, 1941, p. 35.

"The Through Service to Red Boiling Springs." *The Nashville Tennessean*, July 9, 1924, p. 7.

"The Woman About Town." *The Nashville Tennessean*, April 11, 1909, p. 3.

"The World's Greatest Physician." *The Nashville Tennessean*, May 4, 1928, p. 10.

"Third Tank Explosion Like Fatal One Reported." *The Nashville Tennessean*, June 24, 1923, p. 12.

"35 Miles an Hour Army Area Speed." *The Nashville Tennessean*, September 6, 1942, p. 7.

"Three Congressmen to Address Carriers." *The Nashville Tennessean*, May 23, 1932, p. 3.

"300 Acres Fine Farmland, Red Boiling Springs at Auction." *The Nashville Tennessean and The Nashville American*, April 5, 1917, p. 16.

"Through Pike from Nashville Possible." *The Nashville Tennessean and The Nashville American*, July 8, 1913, p. 2.

"Through Service." *The Nashville Tennessean and The Nashville American*, June 7, 1015, p. 15.

"Tire Lost." *The Nashville Tennessean*, August 20, 1927, p. 12.

"To Benefit the Red Cross." *The Nashville Tennessean*, and *The Nashville American*, August 17, 1917, p. 2.

"To Erect Bridge." *The Nashville Tennessean*, March 1, 1930, p. 3.

"To Honor Byrnes." *The Nashville Tennessean*, November 12, 1933, p. 18.

"To Talk on Weed Signup." *The Nashville Tennessean*, December 10, 1934, p. 13.

"Tours Set by Candidates." *The Nashville Tennessean*, June 20, 1938, pp. 1-2.

"T. P. A. Members at Red Boiling Springs." *The Nashville Tennessean*, August 1, 1920, p. D-5.

"Travel Opportunities." *The Nashville Tennessean*, August 13, 1942, p. 18.

"Travel Opportunities." *The Nashville Tennessean*, March 17, 1929, p. 26.

"Trio of Golden Gloves Champions Lose Crowns." *The Nashville Tennessean*, February 12, 1935, p. 10.

"Trip to Standing Stone Forest in Overton and Clay Counties Offers Scenic Delights to Motorists." *The Nashville Tennessean*, May 29, 1938, p. 24.

"Truck Bus Men Organize Here." *The Nashville Tennessean*, February 4, 1927, p. 16.

"12 Bouts Set Monday Night at Hippodrome." *The Nashville Tennessean*, December 13, 1936, p. 13.

"28 Rounds of Boxing at Red Boiling Springs." *The Nashville Tennessean*, August 27, 1927, p. 10.

"Twenty-one Hotels Get Certificates of Good Character." *The Nashville Tennessean and The Nashville American*, September 10, 1916, p. B-13.

"26 Teams Entered in 10th District Meet." *The Nashville Tennessean*, February 18, 1934, p. 11.

"Two Charters Granted." *The Nashville American*, May 11, 1901, p. 10.

"Under Foreclosure Decree." *The Nashville American*, June 17, 1906, p. 5.

Underground Fairyland Exists in Tennessee Caves." *The Nashville Tennessean*, October 11, 1936, p. 38.

"Up-Cumberland Doctors Meet." *The Nashville Tennessean*, June 9, 1927, p. 14.

"Upper Cumberland Medicos End Annual Meet at Springs." *The Nashville Tennessean*, June 18, 1936, p. 5.

"Upper Tennessee Medicos to Meet." *The Nashville Tennessean*, June 14, 1931, p. 5.

"Upper Cumberland Road Conference to be Held." *The Nashville Tennessean*, July 10, 1927, p. 28.

"Vacation." *The Nashville Tennessean*, August 1, 1940, p. 11.

"Vacation Rates." *The Nashville Tennessean and The Nashville American*, May 25, 1915, p. 2.

"Vacation Time." *The Nashville Tennessean*, May 31, 1926, p. 5.

"Valley Head May Speak." *The Nashville Tennessean*, July 6, 1933, p. 10.

"Votes of Tyson in Senate Compiled." *The Nashville Tennessean*, June 30, 1927, p. 8.

"Want a Bridge." *The Nashville American*, March 10, 1903, p. 9.

"Wanted Male and Female." *The Nashville Tennessean and The Nashville American*, May 13, 1915, p. B-10.

"Wanted." *The Nashville American*, April 16, 1902, p. 5.

"Wanted. *The Nashville American*, September 7, 1901, p. 5.

"Wanted." *The Nashville American*, June 16, 1901, p. 18.

"Wanted." *The Nashville American*, June 21, 1905, p. 5.

"Wanted." *The Nashville Tennessean and The Nashville American*, September 12,1914, p. C-11.

"Wants Baseball Games." *The Nashville Tennessean*, June 17, 1927, p. 11.

"Wants Game." *The Nashville Tennessean*, August 12, 1927, p. 11.

Warden, Margaret Lindsley. "Horse Sense." *The Nashville Tennessean*, February 19, 1939, p. 14.

Watkins, R. H. "Mineral Waters of the Country." *The Nashville American*, August 10, 1906, p. 2.

Watson, C. C. "Rush to the Summer Resorts Near Nashville." *The Nashville American*, August 11, 1907, p. A-7.

"Weekly Editors to Meet at Red Boiling Springs." *The Nashville Tennessean*, June 11, 1937, p. 5.

"Well Known Man Here." *The Nashville Tennessean and The Nashville American*, June 18, 1914, p. 14.

"Wesley Alumni to Hold Reunion." *The Nashville Tennessean*, May 24, 1950, p. 57.

"White and Stone Open Campaign in Livingston Today." *The Nashville Tennessean*, September 15, 1926, p. 1.

"White Makes Excellent Run to Red Boiling Springs." *The Nashville Tennessean and The Nashville American*, August 30, 1914, p. D-2.

"Who's Who in Nashville Business World." *The Nashville Tennessean*, April 14, 1930, p. 8.

"Will Honor Byrns." *The Nashville Tennessean*, October 29, 1933, p. 12.

"Willow Grove Dr. Upper Cumberland Chief." *The Nashville Tennessean*, June 17, 1926, p. 2.

"Win School Honors." *The Nashville Tennessean*, May 9, 1941, p. 24.

"With Kennedy Brothers." *The Nashville Tennessean and The Nashville American*, February 9, 1913, p. B-7.

"Wm. B. Brewer." *The Nashville Tennessean*, September 8, 1908, p. 7.

"Woman and Society." *The Nashville American*, August 7, 1907, p. 5.

"Woman's Department." *The Nashville American*, August 11, 1907, p. 15.

"Work of Surveyors Excites Citizens." *The Nashville Tennessean*, June 21, 1907, p. 2.

"Yessir ... Rusco S. S." *The Nashville Tennessean*, April 12, 1928, p. 8.

About the Author

CL Gammon has had a life-long fascination with the written word. This fascination has led to his authoring more than 70 books.

Over the years, Gammon, who studied Political Science at Tennessee Technological University and History and Government at Hillsdale College, has been the recipient of several prestigious honors and awards. Some of the honors he has received are the Certificate of Appreciation for Service to the State of Tennessee, the Partisan Prohibition Historical Society Citation of Merit (the only two-time recipient), and nomination for the 2023 Gilder Lehrman Lincoln Prize.

Several universities, including the State University of New York, the University of Akron, and East Mississippi Community College, have utilized his books as course material.

Articles written by Gammon have appeared in more than a dozen national and regional publications. He has also written feature articles for his hometown newspaper, *The Macon County Times*.

CL Gammon lives in Lafayette, Tennessee.

www.ingramcontent.com/pod-product-compliance
Lightning Source LLC
Chambersburg PA
CBHW060741050426
42449CB00008B/1284